银行英语

Banking English

赵世刚 主编

北京大学出版社
PEKING UNIVERSITY PRESS

图书在版编目(CIP)数据

银行英语 / 赵世刚主编. —北京：北京大学出版社，2007.11
ISBN 978-7-301-12729-2

Ⅰ.银… Ⅱ.赵… Ⅲ.银行业务–英语–口语 Ⅳ.H319.9

中国版本图书馆 CIP 数据核字(2007)第 139646 号

书　　　名：	银行英语
著作责任者：	赵世刚　主编
责 任 编 辑：	刘　强
封 面 设 计：	福瑞来书装
标 准 书 号：	ISBN 978-7-301-12729-2/H·1839
出 版 发 行：	北京大学出版社
地　　　址：	北京市海淀区成府路 205 号　100871
网　　　址：	http://www.pup.cn
电　　　话：	邮购部 62752015　发行部 62750672
	编辑部 62767347　出版部 62754962
电 子 邮 箱：	liuqiang@pup.pku.edu.cn
印 刷 者：	北京汇林印务有限公司
经 销 者：	新华书店
	650 毫米×980 毫米　16 开本　17.75 印张　273 千字
	2007 年 11 月第 1 版　2008 年 6 月第 2 次印刷
定　　　价：	32.00 元（配有光盘）

未经许可，不得以任何方式复制或抄袭本书之部分或全部内容。
版权所有，侵权必究　举报电话：010-62752024
电子邮箱：fd@pup.pku.edu.cn

主编
　　赵世刚

编委
　　白兰平　祖　梅　福　萍　范守智
　　杜　超　赵　君　张吉新　陈　宇

编辑
　　张东梅　姚　恪　韩晔辉

校对
　　张东梅　姚　恪　张　超　赵　婷　贾宝莹

撰稿人员（以姓氏笔画为序）
　　马晓蕊　亢　锦　尹朝霞　田　园　朱　旷　刘长广
　　刘　旸　刘　莹　刘　靖　刘　巍　孙璐璐　李　克
　　李　凯　李　波　李　虹　李慧凝　李　震　吴自林
　　吴　静　何　箐　汪艾雪　张　红　张丽丽　张纹纹
　　张　超　张　靖　张赛怡　陈　丹　陈　净　陈　静
　　赵　红　赵　琳　赵博文　赵　雯　赵　婷　侯亚娜
　　侯　悦　姚　恪　姚　娟　袁卫华　高　原　郭小岛
　　郭融晖　黄　洁　崔　佳　傅轶斌　裴　方　潘雁蕊

银行英语
Banking English

前　言

　　2008年北京奥运会是中华民族的伟大盛事，是展示中华民族新面貌、新形象的巨大舞台。中国银行作为北京2008年奥运会唯一银行合作伙伴，将为北京2008年奥运会、残奥会及其系列测试赛期间来自世界各地的运动员、教练员、体育官员、记者和游客提供快捷、周到、方便的银行服务。

　　以中国银行在奥运会期间接待这些外宾客户办理银行业务为背景，我们编写了这本实用《银行英语》教材，旨在帮助读者全面提高银行英语口语对话能力，系统掌握有关银行柜台业务的基本知识。

　　本书来源于银行一线，服务于银行一线，侧重口语能力提高，通过情景对话的形式，将奥运会特定内容与日常接待服务有机结合，可以用于奥运会金融服务人员英语口语强化训练，实用性和针对性很强；本书内容涉及银行经常为外宾客户办理的各项个人业务，贴近实际，能够满足银行从业人员在日常工作中实际运用英语的需要，可以用于金融同业进行银行英语培训，同时也是高等院校财经类专业师生掌握银行英语的一条捷径，适用性和通用性较高。

　　本书共七个部分，五十七个单元，主要内容包括本外币存取款、外币兑换、旅行支票、境内外汇款、信用卡、保管箱、大堂经理咨询、奥运会门票销售等。

　　由于时间仓促，疏漏之处在所难免，欢迎读者批评指正。

中国银行股份有限公司北京市分行
二〇〇七年十月二十八日

目 录

第一部分 存取款业务
Part I Deposit and Withdrawal Service

第一单元	开立活期账户 ……………………………	2
	Opening a Current Account …………………	3
第二单元	开立定期存款账户 ………………………	8
	Opening a Time Deposit Account …………	9
第三单元	存款及定期提前支取 ……………………	12
	Making Deposit and Early Withdrawal ……	13
第四单元	活期存款转定期存款二例 ………………	16
	Two Examples of Transferring from Savings Account to Time Deposit Account …………	17
第五单元	关户及密码挂失 …………………………	20
	Closing an Account and Reporting Loss of the PIN Number ………………………………	21
第六单元	存单挂失及取款透支 ……………………	24
	Reporting Loss of the Deposit Certificate and Overdrawing ………………………………	25
第七单元	借记卡挂失二例 …………………………	28
	Two Examples of Loss Report of Debit Cards …………………………………	29
第八单元	指导使用自助提款机 ……………………	32
	How to Use the ATM ………………………	33
第九单元	指导在自助存款机存款 …………………	36
	How to Use the Cash Deposit Machine (CDM) ………………………………	37
补充单词	……………………………………………	40
Exercise	……………………………………………	40

Banking English

第二部分　外币兑换
Part II　Foreign Currency Exchange

第一单元　外币兑换一般手续 …………………… 44
General Procedures for Foreign Currency Exchange ………………………………… 45

第二单元　保管兑换水单 ……………………… 48
Keeping the Exchange Memo …………… 49

第三单元　收取手续费规定 ……………………… 52
The Charge Standard for Foreign Currency Exchange ………………………………… 53

第四单元　非居民兑换外币 ……………………… 56
Non-Residents Purchasing Foreign Currency ……………………………… 57

第五单元　外币兑换二例 ……………………… 60
Two Examples of Foreign Currency Exchange ………………………………… 61

第六单元　解释为何没收假钞 …………………… 64
Explanations about Confiscating Counterfeit Note ……………………………… 65

第七单元　介绍假币的一般特征和没收假币的手续 …… 66
General Features of Counterfeit Notes and Confiscation Procedures ………………… 67

补充单词 ……………………………………… 70
Exercise ……………………………………… 70

第三部分　旅行支票
Part III　Traveler's Cheques

第一单元　咨询旅行支票托收 …………………… 74
Inquiring about Traveler's Cheques Collection ………………………………… 75

第二单元　复签、贴息及买卖差价 ……………… 78
Countersignature, Discount and Cash Withdrawal Charge ……………………… 79

第三单元　当面复签及不可代兑旅支 …………… 82
Countersigning in the Presence of the Bank Clerk and Cashing in Person ………… 83

Contents

第四单元	旅支授权及保管水单 ……………	86
	Authorization and Exchange Memo …………	87
第五单元	旅支复签及现钞面额 ………………	88
	Countersigning and Asking for Various Banknote Denominations …………	89
第六单元	旅行支票丢失处理 ………………	92
	Solutions to Lost or Stolen Traveler's Cheques …………	93
第七单元	旅行支票不得代签及背书转让 ……………	96
	Countersigning Your Own Traveler's Cheques …………	97
补充单词	…………………………………	100
Exercise	…………………………………	100

第四部分 汇款业务
Part Ⅳ Remittance

第一单元	咨询海外汇款 ………………	104
	Checking Inward Remittance …………	105
第二单元	汇款手续费与定期自动转存 ……………	108
	Remittance Commission and Making a Time Deposit …………	109
第三单元	汇入查询二例 ………………	112
	Two Examples of Checking Inward Remittance …………	113
第四单元	解释汇款名称不符的问题 ……………	116
	Dealing with Non-Compliance of Account Name and Number …………	117
第五单元	合格汇票的兑付与托收 ……………	120
	Cashing and Collection of a Bank Draft …………	121
第六单元	非居民客户向海外汇款 ……………	126
	Outward Remittance by Non-Residents ……	127
第七单元	汇出汇款业务操作与填单辅导 ……………	130
	Remittance Operation and Guiding Customers with Application …………	131

银行英语
Banking English

第五部分　信用卡业务
Part V　Credit Card

第一单元	申请中银长城国际卡 ……………………	136
	Applying for a BOC Great Wall International Card ……………	137
第二单元	办理中银信用卡 …………………………	140
	Applying for a BOC Credit Card …………	141
第三单元	申请长城人民币信用卡 …………………	146
	Applying for a BOC Great Wall Domestic Card ………………………………	147
第四单元	信用卡一般取现手续 ……………………	150
	Procedures for Cash Withdrawal with a Credit Card ………………………………	151
第五单元	外卡取现/授权要求 ……………………	154
	Cash Withdrawal/Authorization Requirements for Foreign Credit Card ………………	155
第六单元	介绍信用卡的类型功能及费率标准 ……	158
	Introduction to Credit Card—Type, Function and Charge Standards …………………	159
第七单元	自动取款机故障 …………………………	162
	When the ATM is Not Working Properly ……………………………	163
第八单元	处理有争议的取现业务 …………………	168
	Dealing with Complaints and Misunderstandings …………………………………	169
第九单元	ATM 机吞卡的处理 ……………………	176
	When the Card is Stuck in the ATM ……	177
第十单元	大堂经理信用卡常识问答 ………………	180
	Questions and Answers about Credit Card …………………………………	181
Exercise	……………………………………………	185

目录
Contents

第六部分　银行保管箱业务
Part VI　Safe Deposit Box

第一单元	介绍开办保管箱业务的分支机构 ……………	188
	Directing Clients to the Right Bank …………	189
第二单元	在中银大厦支行开立保管箱 …………………	192
	Opening a Safe Deposit Box at Zhong Yin Da Sha Sub-Branch ………………………………	193
第三单元	开箱及续租 ……………………………………	198
	Opening a Box and Extending the Lease ……	199
第四单元	挂失及解挂 ……………………………………	202
	Reporting Loss and Replacing the Keys ……	203
第五单元	退箱 ……………………………………………	206
	Returning the Safe Deposit Box ……………	207
第六单元	全自动保管箱业务手续 ………………………	210
	Automatic Safe Deposit Box Services in Bank of China ……………………………	211
补充单词	…………………………………………………	214
Exercise	…………………………………………………	214

第七部分　大堂经理咨询服务
Part VII　Questions and Answers at the Inquiry Desk

第一单元	大堂经理致欢迎词 ……………………………	218
	Making a Welcoming Speech ………………	219
第二单元	介绍中国银行历史及标识 ……………………	220
	A Brief History of the Bank of China and Its Logo ………………………………………	221
第三单元	介绍营业时间和营业网点 ……………………	224
	Telling Customers about Business Hours and Offices ………………………………………	225
第四单元	银行员工引导客户 ……………………………	226
	Ushering-in ……………………………………	227
第五单元	叫号机的使用与银行突发事件的解释和处理 ………………………………	230
	Using Ticket Station and Handling Emergencies …………………………………	231

银行英语
Banking English

第六单元	接待友好客户并回答相关奥运问题 …………	234
	Receiving Friendly Customers and Answering Questions about Olympic Games …………	235
第七单元	接待着急客户 ……………………………	238
	Receiving a Worried Customer ……………	239
第八单元	为残疾运动员提供特殊服务 ………………	240
	Providing Customized Services for Disabled Athletes ………………………………	241
补充单词	………………………………………………	244
Exercise	………………………………………………	244

补充阅读资料
Supplementary Reading

第一单元	解释奥运会门票售票办法-1 ………………	248
	Explanations about the Olympic Ticketing Policies-1 ……………………………	249
第二单元	解释奥运会门票售票办法-2 ………………	252
	Explanations about the Olympic Ticketing Policies-2 ……………………………	253
第三单元	奥运英语竞赛 ……………………………	256
	Olympic English Contest ……………………	257
补充单词	………………………………………………	264
Exercise	………………………………………………	264

附 录
Appendix

附录一	可兑换外币表 ……………………………	265
	Convertible Foreign Currencies ……………	265
附录二	国内外主要银行机构表 …………………	266
	The Primary Domestic and Foreign Banking Institutions …………………………	266

Keys ……………………………………………………… 267

第一部分 存取款业务
Part I Deposit and Withdrawal Service

Banking English

存取款业务—1

开立活期账户

银行存款主要包括两大类,活期存款和定期存款。长城电子借记卡是中国银行现代化个人理财工具的标志性产品,一直以来都受到国内外客户的喜爱。一位外国客户在听取柜员关于中国银行各种存款产品的介绍之后决定开立一个活期账户,并且要求将账户勾连一张长城借记卡。

T: 柜员 C: 客户

T: 早上好,先生,请问您需要什么帮助吗?
C: 你好,我想开个账户,请问如何办理?
T: 我行提供活期和定期两种账户。
C: 请问这两种账户都有什么特点呢?
T: 活期储蓄账户可以随时存取款,人民币起存金额为1元,外币乙种存款起存金额为人民币100元的等值外币;而定期账户有不同的固定期限。
C: 我是特地为奥运会而来的,同时我也要去其他的城市,所以我想开一个活期账户,可以在全国存取款。

Deposit and Withdrawal Service

Opening a Current Account

Unit 1

Bank deposits are usually in two forms: demand deposits and time deposits. The Great Wall Electronic Debit Card, a classic symbol of Bank of China's modern personal financing tools, is an all-time-favorite for numerous customers at home and abroad. Now a customer decides to open a current account linked with the Great Wall debit card after a bank teller explains to him the different features of the accounts offered by Bank of China.

T: Teller   C: Customer

T: Good morning, Sir! Is there anything I can do for you?

C: Good morning. I'd like to open an account. Would you please tell me how to do it?

T: Certainly. We have both current accounts and time deposit accounts.

C: Could you tell me the differences between the two?

T: A current account takes the form of a bank passbook with which you can make deposits and withdrawals any time you want without setting the maturity date of your deposits. The minimum initial deposit for opening a current account is 1 Chinese Yuan or 100 Yuan worth of foreign currency. Unlike the current account, the time deposit account does not allow you to withdraw anytime you want, and there is a fixed maturity date for each deposit.

C: I have come for the Olympic Games. Besides, I will visit other cities while I am in China. So, I want to open an account that I can use anywhere in China.

account /əˈkaʊnt/ n. 账户, 账目
deposit /dɪˈpɒzɪt/ v. 存款, 存放, 堆积
　　　n. 存款, 定金, 堆积物
maturity /məˈtʃʊərɪti/ n. (票据)到期
minimum /ˈmɪnɪməm/ n. 最小值, 最低(程度)
　　　adj. 最小的, 最低的
withdraw /wɪðˈdrɔː/ v. 支取, 收回

银行英语
Banking English

T: 我明白了,我们有一种"长城电子借记卡",非常适合您的需求,它可以在全国范围内取款、存款和购物消费。如果您感兴趣,我们今天就可帮您办理。请问您带护照了吗?

C: 带了,给你。

T: 请您填写一份开户申请书,将您的个人信息填写清楚。为方便您通过电话查询余额或进行资金转账,建议您可以开通电话银行服务功能。

C: 写好了,给您。

T: 谢谢。

C: 请问有手续费吗?

T: 有的。每年会自动扣划10元的年费。开卡有5元开卡费,开户最低存款额为1元。

T: 请先输入六位存折密码,连续输两遍。好了,现在您可以设置借记卡密码,请连输两遍。若您申请电话银行,只要再输入两遍电话银行密码就可以了。

T: 都做好了,这个是您的存折,可以在北京的中国银行任一家网点柜台存取款;这是您的卡,可以在全国使用。我还必须提醒您一点,在这个账户中,只有人民币可以在全国存取。

C: 你的意思是在这个存折中,我只能在北京用外币,其他的城市不行吗?

中国银行股份有限公司北京分行
Bank of China Limited Beijing Branch

Deposit and Withdrawal Service

T: I see. Our Great Wall Debit Card is a good choice for you. You can use the card for cash deposit or withdrawal in any Bank of China office all over China, and you can go shopping with it too. If you are interested in it, we can issue this card for you today, and you can get the card immediately. Now could you please show me your passport?

C: Certainly. Here you are.

T: Please fill out this application form to open an account. Make sure your personal information is clear and accurate. Furthermore, you'd better open a telephone banking service which is convenient for you to check the balance or make transfers.

C: OK. Here you are.

T: Thank you.

C: Any charge for opening this account?

T: The annual fee of the card is 10 Yuan, but you don't have to pay it today, it will be automatically deducted from your account every year. What you should pay today is five Yuan as the cost of the new card plus at least 1 Yuan as your account's initial deposit.

T: Please enter a 6-digit pin number for your account book... again, please... Now you can set a password for your debit card. Please enter the password twice. If you want to open a telephone banking service, you also need to enter the password twice.

T: Well, everything is OK now. Here is your passbook. You can use it to deposit or withdraw money in any Bank of China sub-branches in Beijing. Here is your card, which can be used not only in Beijing, but also in other provinces of China. And before you go, some tips about this card, if you use the card in other provinces, you can only make RMB transactions.

C: You mean that I can only make foreign currency transactions in Beijing with this card, but not elsewhere in China, right?

withdrawal /wɪðˈdrɔːəl/ n. 支取
passport /ˈpɑːspɔːt/ n. 护照
accurate /ˈækjurət/ adj. 精确的,准确的
automatically /ˌɔːtəˈmætɪkli/ adv. 自动地
deduct /dɪˈdʌkt/ v. 扣除
afterwards /ˈɑːftəwədz/ adv. 以后,随后

Banking English

T： 是的。您可以到北京中行任一网点来随时更新存折记录,您卡上的每一笔交易都会在存折上反映出来。

C： 噢,我明白了,太感谢你了!

T： 不客气。

C： 再见!

T： 再见!

NOTES

1. Is there anything I can do for you?/What can I do for you?/May I help you? 这三句话的意思是"需要帮忙吗?"或"有什么事情吗?",是最基本的商业用语。一般国外经常用:How can I help you?

2. open an account/ set up an account 开户

3. a 6-digit pin number 六位数字的密码。 密码的表达方式很多,柜台上经常使用的有 password, code, secret code, pin number 等。但由于"password"在发音上有些像"passport(护照)"以及" passbook(存折)",在柜台交流时可能会造成不必要的误会,造成多余的解释工作。因此建议使用"pin number"等词。同样的问题也会在 passbook 上出现。对于"存折",passbook 当然是很好的翻译,但或许是由于上文提到的发音近似的缘故,或许是因为部分国家的客户对"存折"的概念并不熟悉,在柜台交流时使用"passbook"有时确实会造成一些小误会。因此,在柜台提到存折的时候,我们可以灵活些,事实上,"the account book"、"the book"、"the account",甚至"the yellow book"等(目前,我行活期一本通存折为黄色封面)虽然都不标准,但却都可以在一定场合用来表达"活期存折"的意思。

4. update,更新信息; update the passbook,登折; update the product profile,更新产品介绍

5. everything,每一件事;anything,任何事
   Anything that we do must be compliant to bank policy. 我们所作的任何事都必须符合银行规定。
   something,有些事 You must be able to do something to solve my problem. 你肯定能做些什么帮助我解决问题。

Deposit and Withdrawal Service

T: Right. By the way, you can update your transaction record at any of our branches in Beijing by presenting this passbook to us. All transaction items of the card will be reflected in this book.
C: Oh, I see. Thanks a lot!
T: You're welcome!
C: Good-bye!
T: Good-bye!

transaction /træn'zækʃən/ n. 交易
update /ʌp'deɪt/ vt. 更新

中国银行股份有限公司北京崇文支行
Bank of China Limited Beijing Chongwen Subbranch

银行英语
Banking English

存取款业务—2

开立定期存款账户

和活期存款不同的是,定期存款的存款人不能随时支取存款,每笔存款都会有固定的到期支取日。当然,一般说来,定期存款的利率都会比活期存款高。如果一个人有一笔钱暂时不会用到,定期存款或许是个很好的选择。现在,一位客户正想在银行开立定期存款账户。让我们来看看他和柜员是如何谈论存期和利率的。

  T: 柜员 C: 客户

T: 下午好。有什么事吗?
C: 是的,我有点钱,现在不用,想在贵行开一个账户。
T: 非常欢迎,我们这儿有不同的存款种类,顺便问一下,不知您预计何时用钱?
C: 一年,至少半年。
T: 您可以选择我们为您提供的定期存款。
C: 存款在账户中储存多久才可以取?
T: 外币定期存款的存款期限一共有1个月、3个月、6个月、一年、两年五个档次。
C: 据我所知,定期存款的利率比活期储蓄存款的利率要高得多。
T: 是的。定期存款存期越长利率越高。
C: 如果我存半年期,利率是多少?
T: 美元年利率2.875%。
T: 我们的大多数顾客选用3个月或6个月存款期限。存款到期时,如果您不支取的话,我们将把您的存款按原定期限自动续存。
C: 那您帮我开个定期账户吧。
T: 可以,您带护照了吗?
C: 带了,给您。
T: 您要选择定期存单还是定期一本通存折呢?
C: 这两者之间有什么差别么?
T: 在账户性质方面没有任何差别,到期后都可以自动转存。只是根据客户喜好不

Deposit and Withdrawal Service

Opening a Time Deposit Account

Unlike the current account, the time deposit account does not allow the depositors to withdraw their money anytime they want, and there is a fixed maturity date for each deposit. But generally, a time deposit gives much higher interest than a current account. If a person has some money that he or she does not intend to spend for the moment, the time deposit may be a good choice. Now a customer wants to open a time deposit account in the bank. Let us see how he and the teller talk about the maturity date and the interest rate.

T: Teller   C: Customer

T: Good afternoon. What can I do for you?

C: Yes, I've got some money that I don't want to use for the moment. I'd like to open an account in your bank.

T: OK, Sir. We offer different deposit products in our bank. By the way, when do you expect to use the money?

C: Maybe one year from now, or at least half a year.

T: Then you can open a time deposit account in our bank.

C: How long do I need to deposit my money in your bank before I can withdraw it?

T: The deposit terms for foreign currency are: one month, three months, six months, one year and two years.

C: I suppose the interest rate for a time deposit is much higher than that of the savings account?

T: That's correct. Besides, the longer the term, the higher the interest rate.

C: What is the interest rate for half a year?

T: The annual interest rate for a six-month U.S. dollar term deposit is 2.875%.

offer /ˈɒfə/ v. 提供

同，我们设计了存单和存折两种账户形式，存单只能存一笔，而一个存折可以至少存60笔。

C：那您先帮我开个存单吧。

T：好的，请您填一份开户申请表……请您连续输入两遍存单密码。

T：给您办好了，您拿好了。

C：谢谢！

T：不客气。

NOTES

1. I suppose the interest rate for time deposit is much higher than that of the savings account? 这句话中的much修饰形容词比较级higher，代词that相当于the interest rate，为了避免重复，故有此表达方式。

2. The longer the term, the higher the interest rate. 此句句型为 The＋形容词比较级……，the＋形容词比较级……，意思是"越……，越……"。例如：The harder you work, the higher score you can get. 你越努力，你的得分就会越高。

3. 银行的存款产品种类很多且不断更新，但总有些固定的说法是我们学习的主干，下面就对一些主要名词进行简单的说明和归类：

   current account：这个词在多数国内的银行中普遍用作"活期账户"解释。提到活期账户，我们就会想到以本外币一本通、长城借记卡为介质的活期储蓄，而一些国外的银行在使用current account时，会把它定义为checking account，即支票账户，这种账户的最大特点就是在支取时使用支票，每位客户在开户时都会得到一个cheque book（支票本），他们会用签发个人支票的方式进行日常支付。此外，国外的current account通常是没有利息的，银行甚至还会收取一定比例的佣金作为替客户维护账户的酬劳。

   savings account：这个词直接翻译过来是"储蓄账户"的意思，其实也就是我们经常说的不设定支取日期，随存随取，并享有一定利息收益的活期存款账户。活期存款通常以存折或是银行卡的形式存在。当然，随着银行理财产品的不断更新，不少银行会把一些带有理财性质的、兼具较高收益和较高流动性的，或是针对特殊客户群的存款账户都归入savings account的范畴之内。

   deposit account：字面上的意思是存款账户，通常指定期存款，即固定存期、固定金额、享有较高利率收益的存款产品，有些银行还会把call account（通知存款）划入deposit account中。

   另外，在柜台能够使用到的用来表示账户性质的词还有：

   joint account 共有账户， term deposit/time deposit/fixed deposit 定期存款，deposit certificate 存单， demand deposit/savings deposit/current deposit 活期存款，overnight deposit 隔夜存款，savings-time optional deposits 定活两便存款, call/notice deposit 通知存款，interest withdrawal on principal deposited 存本取息， small savings for lump-sum withdrawal 零存整取，deposit by correspondence 通信存款等。

   我国的存单为deposit certificate，记名，且不可自由转让，国外的大额定期存单为certificate of deposit (CD) 不记名，可自由转让。

Deposit and Withdrawal Service

T: The most popular terms are 3 months or 6 months. If you do not withdraw your money upon maturity, your principal plus the interest will be automatically renewed according to the same deposit term you select today.

C: OK. Please open a time deposit account for me.

T: Certainly. Could you please show me your passport?

C: Here you are.

T: Do you prefer a passbook or a deposit certificate?

C: What is the difference?

T: They are the same, technically, you know, in terms of compound interest, automatic renewal upon maturity... They are just the two forms of the time deposit to meet different needs of customers. If you choose a passbook, you can make up to 60 deposits, and all your transactions will be posted in the passbook; while if you choose a certificate, it will be used for only one transaction of the time deposit.

C: OK. The certificate works for me.

T: Please fill in an application form first... Please enter you password twice.

T: Everything is OK now. Here is your deposit certificate.

C: Thank you!

T: My pleasure!

中国银行股份有限公司北京通州支行
Bank of China Limited Beijing Tongzhou Subbranch

存取款业务—3

存款及定期提前支取

一位女士从法国归来,想将没有用完的现金存入银行。

T: 柜员   C: 客户

T: 下午好,女士。我能为您做些什么?
C: 下午好。我想在我的账户上存些钱。
T: 您想存多少?
C: 2050欧元。这是我的存折和现金。
T: 对不起,您多给了我100欧元,您要不要再数一下。
C: 谢谢!我不数了,那就都存上吧。
T: 好的。(办完手续)请您核对一下存款凭证上打印的金额,如没有问题,就请您在这张凭证上签字。给您存折,请拿好。
C: 好。谢谢。
T: 不用谢。再见。
C: 再见!

一位女士需要一笔钱急用,所以她决定在定期存款到期之前把钱取出来。

T: 柜员   C: 客户

T: 您好。请问您需要什么帮助吗?
C: 我想取一笔钱,应付急用。但是,我原来存的是定期,现在还没有到期。您看怎么办?能够提前支取吗?
T: 当然可以。如果需要的话,您可以提前支取您的存款。但是,在这种情况下,您不能获得原定利息。只有当存单到期,原来约定的存单利率才能生效。

Deposit and Withdrawal Service

Making Deposit and Early Withdrawal

A lady has just come back from France. She wants to deposit some unused Euros in the bank.

T: Teller   C: Customer

T: Good afternoon, Madam. What can I do for you?
C: Good afternoon, I'd like to put some money in my account.
T: How much would you like to put in?
C: Two thousand and fifty Euros. Here is my passbook and the money.
T: Excuse me. You gave me an extra 100 Euro note. Would you count the money again?
C: No, thank you. I don't need to check it again. Anyway, please deposit it all.
T: OK. (...finished) Please double check the amount on the deposit slip. If it is correct, please sign your name on it. Here is your passbook.
C: OK. Thanks.
T: You are welcome. Goodbye.
C: Bye-bye.

A lady needs some money for an emergency, so she decides to withdraw money before her time deposit matures.

T: Teller   C: Customer

T: Hello. May I help you?
C: Yes, I need some cash right now. But I only have a time deposit. What can I do? Can I take money out before it matures?
T: Yes, you can withdraw your money by cashing the certificate before the maturity. But you would not receive the stated interest. The higher rate is applied only if the certificate is kept for the full term of the deposit.

C: 您的意思是说,我会失去所有的利息?
T: 不,不是全部的,由于您提前取款,我们要根据活期利率标准付给您利息。
C: 那么利率应是多少呢?
T: 目前,美元活期利率是1.15%,其他期限的存款利率表,您可以看一下我们大厅的电子显示屏。
C: 那么您是说,如果我在定期存单到期日之前不得不兑现的话,我就要为此而受到损失。
T: 是这样的。这就是为什么我们希望顾客在承诺定期存款之前,应认真地选择存款期限。
C: 谢谢您。为了急用,我只好将5000美元定期,提前支取3000美元。
T: 对了。您定期剩余的2000美元还按定期利率计算。不过部分提前支取只限一次。
C: 原来是这样。谢谢您的提示。
T: 给您。请清点好。
C: 谢谢!再见!
T: 再见!

NOTES

1. You would not receive the stated interest. 意思是"你拿不到规定的利息"。the stated interest 意为存单上标明的利息。

2. 关于存折/存单上的内容,有一些词语在交流中会反复出现,例如:depositor 存款人, account holder 账户持有人, account number 账号, opening bank 开户行, issue date 存单/折签发日, passbook/certificate number 存单/折号, authorized signature/seal 银行签章, balance 余额, interest rate 利率, interest tax 利息税, time of deposit 存入日, time of withdrawal 支取日, term/period of deposit 存期, maturity/due date 到期日, operator number 柜员(经办)号码等。

14

Deposit and Withdrawal Service

C: You mean I would lose all my interest?

T: Not exactly. If you make an early withdrawal, the interest will be calculated at the rate of a regular savings account.

C: What is that rate?

T: The savings account rate for US dollars is 1.15% now, and the rates for other deposits are all shown on the electronic screen in the lobby.

C: Are you telling me that I have to give up the higher interest if I want to cash my certificate before the due date?

T: Yes, that's right. That is also why we always tell the clients to select a proper deposit term before they open an account.

C: Thank you. But I do need the money. Now here is the 5,000 dollars deposit certificate, and I really have to take 3,000 dollars out of it.

T: Oh, in that case, the remaining 2,000 dollars shall continue to bear interest at the rate of the time deposit as stated before. But you can only do partial withdrawal once. Next time, if you still want to withdraw some money before the maturity date, you have to make a full withdrawal.

C: Thank you for your advice.

T: Here is the money. Please have a double check.

C: Thanks. Good-bye.

T: Bye-bye.

银行英语
Banking English

存取款业务—4

活期存款转定期存款二例

现在,越来越多的人开始接受"理财"这一概念。如果人们手头有一些闲钱,他们或许会用于个人投资,或许会参与商业银行的各类理财计划。从某种意义上讲,定期存款是一种最为基本的理财产品,它并不需要什么高深的投资知识或是敏锐的市场感觉,而且绝大多数商业银行都经营定期存款业务。下面就是两个关于在中国银行开立定期存款账户的例子。

T: 柜员　　C: 客户

例1

T: 您好,请问您办理什么业务?
C: 你好,在我的活期账户中有一些钱,但是我现在暂时不用,你们有没有定期存款?
T: 有的,我们可以给您开立一个新的定期一本通账户。您的护照带了吗?
C: 带了,给你。
T: 您想存多少钱?多长时间?
C: 50000元,3个月。
T: 好的。
T: 办理好了。这是您的定期一本通账户,在北京的中国银行都可以使用。
C: 很感谢,再见。
T: 欢迎再来,再见!

Two Examples of Transferring from Savings Account to Time Deposit Account

Now more and more people have begun to embrace the idea of "wealth management". If people get some money to which they don't need instant access, they would either make an investment in the market or engage in wealth management programs offered by commercial banks. The time deposit, to some extent, is a basic means of wealth management. It does not require much investment knowledge or sharp market awareness; plus, it is very popular in most commercial banks. Here are two examples about opening a time deposit account in the Bank of China.

T: Teller   C: Customer

Example One

T: Good afternoon, what can I do for you?

C: Good afternoon! I have some money in my savings account and I won't use it for a while. Do you have time deposit service?

T: Yes. We can open a time deposit account for you. Do you have your passport with you?

C: Yes, here you are!

T: How much do you want to deposit? And for how long?

C: Fifty thousand Yuan for three months.

T: OK!

T: This is your "Passbook of Time Deposit Account", and you can use it in any Bank of China branches in Beijing.

C: Thank you very much. Bye!

T: See you!

银行英语 Banking English

例 2

T: 您好,请问您办理什么业务?
C: 我要把活期存折上的人民币存成定期存单。
T: 好的。请先给我您的活期存折和护照。
C: 好的。
T: 请问您要转存定期的金额和期限。
C: 5000元人民币存半年。
T: 好的,先要从您的活期存折中取款,请您输入存折密码。
C: 好。
T: 请问您新开的存单要设置密码吗?如果要密码请输入存单密码。
C: 好。密码同样是六位吗?
T: 是的。
C: 输好了。
T: 您的业务办理完了,请您收好您的护照和存单、存折。
C: 谢谢!再见!
T: 再见!

NOTES

1. be made up of 由……组成
   e.g. Is the code made up of 6 digits? 密码是六位数字组成的吗?
   e.g. The team is made up of financial experts from all over China.
   这个小组的成员全是来自中国各地的金融专家。

2. set up a new password 设定新密码

3. regular 表示常规
   exotic 表示非常规,如 exotic financial derivatives 非常规金融衍生工具

4. branch,银行的分支机构,此外,我们经常讲的银行网点还可以用 outlet 来表示。

Deposit and Withdrawal Service

Example Two

T: Hello, can I help you?

C: I want to transfer the money from my regular savings account to a time deposit certificate.

T: Certainly! Can I have your sawings account passbook and the passport please?

C: Sure.

T: How much would you like to transfer?

C: Five thousand Yuan for half a year.

T: OK. First we need to withdraw the money from your savings account, please enter your password.

C: OK!

T: Would you like to set up a new password for this time deposit account? If yes, please enter the new code.

C: Sure! Is it made up of 6 digits, too?

T: Yes, it is.

C: All right!

T: Everything is OK now! Please keep your passport, the deposit certificate and the passbook.

C: Thank you! Goodbye!

T: My pleasure! Bye!

transfer /træns'fɜː/ v. 转移，调转，汇划

银行英语
Banking English

存取款业务—5

关户及密码挂失

一位来中国参加奥运会的运动员结束了比赛，准备回国，临行前决定撤销在中行开立的储蓄账户。

T: 柜员　　C: 客户

T： 您好！请问您办什么业务？
C： 我想撤消我的储蓄存款账户。
T： 顺便说一句，每天提取外币现钞的限额是一万美元。如果您需要提取超过限额的现钞，您需要挟带本人有效护照和提钞用途的证明材料去当地外管局进行备案，您凭外管局核发的《提取现钞备案表》和您的有效护照，来我行办理取现手续。而且，请您提前一天通知银行您要提取超过一万美元的现钞。
C： 我知道了。不过手续太复杂了。我今天取8000美元吧，明天再来清户。
T： 好的，这是您的8000美元,请清点。
C： 没错,谢谢。
T： 不客气,再见。
C： 再见！

一位先生在观看奥运会后准备回国,临行前准备取一些现金备用。但遗憾的是，他忘记了存折的密码，现在，他不得不先办理挂失手续了。

Deposit and Withdrawal Service

Closing an Account and Reporting Loss of the PIN Number

Unit 5

An athlete of the Olympic Games has finished his match. He is preparing to go back to his own country. Before leaving China, he decides to close his savings account.

T: Teller   C: Customer

T: Hello. How can I help you?
C: I'd like to close my savings account with your bank.
T: By the way, the daily limit for cash withdrawal is 10,000 U.S. dollars. If you need to withdraw more than this, you must go to the State Administratin of Foreign Exchange with your valid passport and the certificte for the usage of the money. Then they will issue a form to you. You need to return to our bank with your passport and the form to do the business. Furthermore, we also need a one-day notice in advance according to the policy of our central bank.
C: I see. But it's too complicated. I'd like to withdraw 8,000 U.S. dollars today. And I will come back to close my account tomorrow. Is it OK?
T: Certainly! This is your 8000 U.S. dollars. Please check it.
C: Correct. Thank you very much.
T: My pleasure! See you.
C: See you.

After watching the 2008 Olympic Games, a gentleman decides to go back to his own country. Before he goes, he wants to get some cash for the journey home. But it turns out that he forgets the pin number of his passbook, and thus he has to go through the procedure of reporting loss first.

Banking English

T: 柜员   C: 客户

T: 早上好,先生。
C: 早上好,我想取些钱。
T: 请问您取多少钱?
C: 3500加元。
T: 请输入您的密码……对不起,您刚才输入的密码不对。请再试一次,好吗?
C: 我已经很久没取过钱了,而且我的账户密码都不同。我再试一次吧。
T: 对不起,还是不对。
C: 可我实在想不起来了。怎么办?
T: 如果您忘记密码的话,那只能办理密码挂失手续,七天之内您暂时无法使用账户资金。但七天之后可以重新设置一个新密码,就可以正常使用账户了。
C: 需要手续费么?
T: 我们需要收取 10 元的密码挂失手续费。
C: 那好吧。那我办理一下挂失手续。
T: 请出示一下您的护照,然后再填一份挂失申请书,把您的个人账户信息填全。
T: 给您办好了,七天之后您带上护照、存折和挂失申请书,来银行重新设置一下新的密码就可以了。
C: 谢谢您。再见。
T: 再见。

NOTES

1. a one-day notice in advance 提前一天通知
2. application form of password loss report 密码挂失申请单
3. put down 相当于 write down,意为"写下、记下",此外"leave"也有类似的意思。

   e.g. Remember to put down all your personal information in the form.
   请把所有的个人信息都写在表格里面。

   e.g. Would you please leave your telephone number here on this paper so that we can contact you?
   麻烦你把电话留在这张纸上,这样我们就能联系到你了。

4. fee 表示手续费,即提供服务所收的费用   fee-based business 为中间业务

Deposit and Withdrawal Service

T: Teller   C: Customer

T: Good morning, Sir.

C: Good morning. I want to withdraw some money.

T: How much would you like to withdraw?

C: Three thousand and five hundred Canadian dollars.

T: Please enter your password... I am sorry. The password you have entered is incorrect. Please try again.

C: I haven't withdrawn money for quite some time, and I have used different passwords for different deposit accounts. Let me try again.

T: I'm sorry, still not correct.

C: Well, I really do not remember the password. What can I do now?

T: If you have forgotten the password, you have to report the loss. We will have your account frozen for seven days, and seven days from now, you can come back to reset the password. Your account can be reactivated at that time.

C: Are there any fees involved?

T: Yes. We charge ten Yuan to handle the loss report.

C: OK then, please do it.

T: Would you show me your passport please? Please fill out this application form for a password loss report; remember to put down all of your personal information in the form.

T: Thank you very much. Seven days from now, you can come back to the bank to reset the password. Make sure you bring your passport, the passbook and this loss report form.

C: Thank you for your help. Bye-bye.

T: Bye-bye.

银行英语
Banking English

存取款业务—6

存单挂失及取款透支

一位外国友人丢失了自己在中国银行开立的存单,十分焦急。他立刻来到中国银行办理存单挂失业务,银行柜员耐心地为他服务。

 T: 柜员　C: 客户

- T: 您好。请问您办理什么业务?
- C: 很抱歉,我的存单丢了。
- T: 请您出示您的证件。您能提供您的存单账号、存款时间、种类、金额,以及您的住址吗?
- C: 可以。
- T: 请您填写挂失申请书。
- C: 填好了。
- T: 请您放心,这笔钱没被取走,现在我们已经把您的存单做挂失处理了。我们要收取您10元挂失手续费。
- C: 好。太感谢了,我还需要做什么?
- T: 七天后,您必须本人来这里办理解除挂失手续,别忘了带上您的证件和挂失申请书。
- C: 非常感谢。再见!
- T: 再见!

一位外国友人来到北京观看奥运会,同时决定在此期间游览北京的名胜古迹。于是,他来到中国银行取款,用来支付这次旅游的支出。

Deposit and Withdrawal Service

Reporting Loss of the Deposit Certificate and Overdrawing

A foreigner has lost his deposit certificate, which he opened in Bank of China. He goes to the bank immediately to report the loss. The bank teller is very patient in serving him.

T: Teller   C: Customer

T: Hello! May I help you?

C: I am sorry, I lost my deposit certificate.

T: Please show me your passport. Could you tell me the details about your deposit certificate, such as the account number, maturity date, deposit type, the amount and your address?

C: Certainly.

T: Please fill out this loss report application form.

C: OK.

T: Don't worry. The money is still in your account and it is safe now. You will need to pay 10 Yuan as the service charge.

C: OK. Thank you so much. Anything else that I have to do?

T: Yes. You should come here to renew the account in seven days. Don't forget to bring your passport and the application form at that time.

C: Thank you! Goodbye!

T: You are welcome! Bye!

renew /rɪ'njuː/ v. 更新,复始,恢复

A foreigner decides to visit some places of historic interest in Beijing. He has some money deposited in Bank of China and now he wants to make a withdrawal.

Banking English

T: 柜员   C: 客户

T： 您好。请问您需要什么帮助吗?
C： 我想取些钱。
T： 好。您准备取多少?
C： 4500英镑。
T： 请输入密码……密码对了,但您的账上只有4020.58英镑。
C： 真的吗?
T： 储蓄账户是不允许透支的。
C： 对不起,我没注意到。
T： 没关系。您可以少取一点。
C： 好吧,那我就取4000英镑吧。
T： 行,再输一遍密码就可以了……这是4000英镑。
C： 非常感谢。
T： 不客气,您还办其他业务吗?
C： 不用了,谢谢,再见。
T： 再见。

NOTES

1. overdraw 透支 通常用在被动句中

   e.g. Your bank account is overdrawn. 你的账户现在透支了。

   e.g. You are 100 dollars overdrawn. 你透支了100美元。

2. Is there anything else I can do for you? 您还办其他业务吗?

   这句话还可以简练地说成"Anything else?"。

3. You should come here to renew the account in seven days. 七天后,您来这里办理解除挂失手续。

   在这里,"七天后"使用了"in seven days"来表达。在表达即将发生的情况或在将来时的句子中,我们可以用"in"加上时间来配合将来的动作。例如：

   e.g. Your meal will be ready in about five minutes.
   您的饭五分钟之后就能做好。

   e.g. He will come and visit your family in two weeks.
   他两周之后来拜访您家。

4. charge 做名词表示费用,做动词表示收费 charge sb. for doing sth. 表示因做某事而向某人收费

Deposit and Withdrawal Service

 T: Teller   C: Customer

T: Hello. Can I help you?

C: I want to withdraw some money.

T: OK. How much do you want to withdraw?

C: 4,500 pounds.

T: Please input your password here... Excuse me, Sir, there is only 4020.58 pounds in your account.

C: Really?

T: I am afraid the savings account is not allowed to be overdrawn.

C: Sorry, I didn't notice that!

T: Never mind. Maybe you would like to withdraw less?

C: All right, then I will withdraw 4,000 pounds.

T: OK. Please enter the password again... Right! Here are the 4,000 pounds.

C: Thank you!

T: My pleasure! Is there anything else I can do for you?

C: No. Thank you, Bye!

T: Bye!

银行英语
Banking English

存取款业务—7

借记卡挂失二例

一直以来,不少人认为银行卡业务凡涉及挂失就会变得很复杂,也很耗费时间。从银行的角度而言,挂失业务主要涉及持卡人身份的核实,手续费解释以及更换新卡等主要工作。而随着计算机系统的逐渐完善,中国银行已经使得借记卡挂失不再是一件难事,客户可以很轻松地完成挂失及补卡手续,及时避免损失。现在,让我们来看一看银行职员是如何帮助一位刚刚丢失了借记卡的客户的。

 T: 柜员　　C: 客户

例1

T: 您好,请问您需要帮忙吗?
C: 是的,我的卡丢了。我恐怕找不到它了,我该怎么办?
T: 那我马上给您办理借记卡挂失,请出示您的护照。
C: 好的,给你。
T: 请您填好这张表格并付15元人民币挂失费用。
C: 好的。
T: 您的挂失手续已经办好了,7个工作日以后请您拿着回单和护照来领取您的新卡。
C: 非常感谢。
T: 不用谢。欢迎您再次光临。
C: 好的,再见。
T: 再见!

例2

T: 您好! 请问您需要帮助吗?

Deposit and Withdrawal Service

Two Examples of Loss Report of Debit Cards

Unit 7

In the past, the loss report procedures of bankcards were generally perceived to be very complicated and time-consuming. From the bank's point of view, the task of loss report mainly involves verification of cardholder's identity, explanation of the bank's commission, and replacement with a new card. With the development of its computer system, Bank of China has made it much more convenient for customers to report loss and avoid risk. Now, let's see how a bank clerk is helping an anxious client who has just lost his card.

T: Teller   C: Customer

Example One

T: Hello. What can I do for you?
C;   Yes. I lost my card. And I'm afraid I can't find it. What shall I do then?
T: OK. I will report the loss of your card immediately. Would you please show me your passport?
C: Sure. Here you are.
T: Now please fill out this form. The charge for loss report is fifteen Yuan.
C: OK.
T: Everything is fine, and your money is safe now. Please come back to collect your new card after seven workdays and please don't forget to bring the receipt I gave you just now and your passport.
C: Thank you very much.
T: You're welcome and hope to see you again!
C: OK. Bye.
T: Bye.

Example Two

T: Hello. How can I help you?

Banking English

C: 您好,今天上午,我的长城卡丢了。
T: 您向我行客户服务中心打电话挂失了吗?
C: 是的,已经挂了,他们告诉我还要到柜台办理一些手续。
T: 您别着急,请出示您的护照。
C: 给您,您能立刻帮我查查今天有没有人用卡取款或消费吗?
T: 好的,您的卡号。
C: 在这里。
T: 请稍等,我给您查一下。沃特森先生,今天您的卡没有取现和消费的记录。如果您发现卡丢失后及时挂失,几乎不会有风险。
C: 这就好了,但愿如此。
T: 请您现在填一份挂失申请单。
C: 好的,多久才能领到新卡?
T: 七天以后,我们要收取您挂失费15元,其中10元是挂失手续费,5元是补制新卡的工本费。
C: 没问题,给您。谢谢,再见。
T: 不客气,再见。

NOTES

1. report loss of the debit card 借用卡挂失
2. go through the procedure 履行程序,注意:proceeding 为法律诉讼,proceeds 为款项 loan proceeds 贷款款项
3. 这里 over the counter 不是 OTC,即场外交易,而是亲自到柜台办理的意思。

Deposit and Withdrawal Service

C: Hello. I lost my Great Wall Card this morning.

T: Have you reported the loss to the call center of BOC?

C: Yes, I have, but I was told to go through some procedures over the counter here.

T: Don't worry. Would you please show me your passport?

C: Here you are. Could you have a quick cheque and see if there's any money missing from my account today?

T: OK, your card number please.

C: Here it is.

T: Please wait a moment and I will cheque it for you. Well, Mr. Watson, there is no withdrawal or consumption record in your account today. You know, if you make the loss report as soon as possible, either by phone or over the counter, your money will be safe.

C: That's good. I hope so.

T: Now please fill out the application form for reporting the loss.

C: OK. But how long will it take to have a new card?

T: Seven days. You will be charged fifteen Yuan: ten Yuan as the loss report charge and five Yuan as the cost of a new card.

C: No problem. Here you are. Thanks and see you next time.

T: You are welcome. See you.

存取款业务—8

指导使用自助提款机

乔治正在给中国银行打电话,询问如何使用 ATM。

 R: 电话座机员　C: 客户

C: 喂。您好,中国银行吗?
R: 欢迎致电中国银行客户服务中心。我是 Elizabeth,请问您需要什么帮助?
C: Elizabeth 你好,我是 George,希望你能帮助我。我从美国来,这是我第一次来到中国,我对周围的情况还不熟。我非常荣幸能够参观北京奥运会,我不仅要看奥运会,在奥运会后,我还要去上海等地看看。我觉得在你们的国家人们使用现金的频率很高,但是在行李里放上大量现金又不太安全,请问出去旅游携带现金的最好办法是什么呢?
R: 没问题。请问您有银行卡吗?
C: 有,我有一张美洲银行的借记卡。
R: 您的卡后面有标志表明这张卡可以使用支付系统,如 **CIRRUS** 和 **PLUS**。您需要将卡上的标志和 ATM 显示的标志匹配,如果有一项匹配的话,您可以用您的卡在那机器上取出你美国账户上的钱。
C: 我不认识中文。那些指示全是中文吗?
R: 我们的机器都是人性化的。它们不仅有中文说明也有英文说明。
C: 那太好了!我可以在机器上取出美元吗?还是只能取人民币?

Deposit and Withdrawal Service

How to Use the ATM

George is calling Bank of China to ask how to use the ATM.

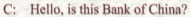

R: Customer Service Representative (CSR)   C: Customer

C: Hello, is this Bank of China?

R: Welcome to telephone customer service center of Bank of China. This is Elizabeth, can I do something for you?

C: How are you, Elizabeth. This is George, I really hope you can help me. I am from America. This is my first time in China, and I'm still not used to life here, yet. It's great though, that I have the opportunity to watch the Olympic Games here in your city. You know, after the Olympics, I also plan to visit some other cities like Shanghai. I know in your country people use cash a lot. But I think having a big stash of cash somewhere in my luggage is not that safe. So can you think of any better way to go traveling around China without worrying about the money issue?

R: Sure. Do you have a bankcard?

C: Yes, I have a debit card issued by this American bank.

R: The logos on your card show that your card can be used by such payment systems as CIRRUS and PLUS. You need to check the logo on the card with the one on the ATMs you might come across during your trip in China. And if the logos match, you can use your card to withdraw money from the ATM whenever you want to.

C: Well, I don't read Chinese, so I am not sure whether I can understand all the Chinese instructions on your ATMs.

R: Don't worry, our ATMs are well-equipped. They have instructions in both Chinese and English.

C: Wonderful. Can I withdraw U.S. dollars or RMB?

Banking English

R: 我们的机器只提供人民币。如果您的账户里有美元存款,建议您先把美元兑换成人民币,这样您在别的城市的ATM机上就能用借记卡取钱了。
C: 好的,我明白了,谢谢你伊丽莎白,你帮了我很大的忙。
R: 没什么,感谢您选择中国银行。再见!
C: 再见!

NOTES

1. though 的用法:though(或是 although)用于对比或转折意思的从句中,表示"虽然、尽管"的意思,有时为了强调,我们通常在 though 前面加上 even,比如:

   She wore a fur coat, even though it was a very hot day. 尽管天气很热,她还是穿了一件裘皮外套。

   需要注意的是,使用 though 或 although 表示"尽管"的意思时,句子中不能再出现"but"或是"yet"等否定词。例如我们想说:尽管他不喜欢数学,但数学考试还是得了90分,就不能说成:Although he doesn't like math, but he got 90 marks in the exam. 而应说成:Although he doesn't like math, he got 90 marks in the exam.

2. compare 的两个词组:compare to 和 compare with

   compare... to... 意为"把……比作",即把两件事物相比较的同时,发现某些方面相似。这两件被比较的事物或人在本质上往往是截然不同的事物。如:

   People usually compare young people to the morning sun.
   人们经常把青年人比作早晨的太阳。

   compare... with... "与……相比,把两件事情相比较,从中找出异同",这两件事又往往是同类的,如:Let me compare my homework with yours. 拿你的作业和我的对比一下。

Deposit and Withdrawal Service

R: Our machines only provide RMB. If you have dollars in your account, you should first change them into RMB here in Beijing so that you can withdraw RMB from the ATMs in other provinces of China.

C: OK, I got it. Thank you very much. I do appreciate your help.

R: You are welcome. Thanks for calling Bank of China. Bye!

C: Bye!

中国银行股份有限公司北京阜成门支行
Bank of China Limited Beijing Fuchengmen Subbranch

存取款业务—9

指导在自助存款机存款

自动存款机是一种提供现金存款和支付的银行自助终端。使用自动存款机方便而且安全,因为交易的每一步都尽在客户的掌握之中。现在,一位客户在使用自动存款机时似乎遇到了些麻烦,他正在向客务中心的银行职员电话求助。

R: 电话座机员 C: 客户

R: 欢迎致电中国银行客服中心,我是戈登。请问您需要什么帮助?
C: 我有个麻烦!我想存钱到我的账户里。但不知为什么机器不能识别我放到存款口里的钱。
R: 钱被存款口卡住了?
C: 是的,我确定,但是我拿不出来。
R: 您能不能试着让机器打印一张收据?
C: 好的,我试试。我打出了收据。
R: 右上方有一个方框上贴着序列号,看到了吗?
C: 我看到了。
R: 请把号码念给我。
C: 号码是44450515。
R: 请稍等,我确定一下您的准确位置。您在北京的分行。您的银行卡号码是多少?
C: 我要按机器上的退出键拿回我的卡,我能这么做吗?
R: 可以。
C: 等一下,好了,我拿回卡了。号码是4321567890123。

Deposit and Withdrawal Service

How to Use the Cash Deposit Machine (CDM)

Unit 9

CDM is a self-service terminal that lets customers make deposits and payment transactions by cash. It is convenient and safe because each transaction step is conducted wholly to the order of customers themselves. Now, a customer seems to have had some trouble with the CDM and he is thus calling the Customer Service Center for help.

R: Customer Service Representative (CSR)   C: Customer

R: Welcome to Bank of China Customer Service Center, Gordon speaking. How can I help you?

C: I have got a problem here. I want to deposit some money into my account, but I don't know why the machine couldn't recognize the money I put in the cash slot. It seems that my account is not credited and the transaction is not confirmed, either.

R: Maybe the cash got stuck inside the slot?

C: Yes, I think so, but I can't get it out.

R: Would you let the machine print out a receipt?

C: Let me try...OK, I got it. I have the receipt.

R: Now just take a look at the receipt. Can you find the box at the upper right of the receipt? There is the serial number of the CDM.

C: Yes. I see it.

R: Would you please read the number for me?

C: The number is "four-four-four-five-zero-five-one-five".

R: Wait a moment please. I'll cheque and confirm your location. OK. You are at a Beijing Branch, and what is your card number?

C: I don't remember. Can I press the exit button on the CDM to get my card back?

R: Yes, you can.

C: Just a moment. OK, I've got my card. The number is 4321567890123.

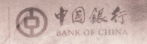

Banking English

R: 请问这卡是哪个银行的?
C: 布赖恩·威廉林。
R: 被卡住了多少钱?
C: 1500元人民币。
R: 我马上跟机器管理人员联系。他们会打电话给你并处理这件事情。在他们跟你联系之前请待在那里别走开。
C: 好的,谢谢你。

机器管理员及时赶到,帮助这位客户解决了问题。

NOTES

1. CDM: cash deposit machine 自动存款机　PUM: passbook update machine 自动登折机
2. straighten out 理清,解决　get the case straightened out 把情况弄清　straighten out the economic order 理顺经济秩序
3. serial number 序号

Deposit and Withdrawal Service

R: Which bank issued your card?
C: Brain Williamson.
R: Do you remember how much money is stuck in the slot?
C: One thousand five hundred Yuan.
R: I will contact the CDM technicians immediately. They will call you directly and help you get things straightened out. Please stay there.
C: OK. Thank you very much.

A CDM technician arrived later, and settled the problem for the customer

Banking English

补充单词

respectively	/rɪ'spektɪvli/	adv.	分别地
maximum	/'mæksɪməm/	n.	最大值,最高(程度)
		adj.	最高的,最多的
available	/ə'veɪləbəl/	adj.	可能的,可用到的;有空的
assume	/ə'sjuːm/	v.	以为,认为
maintain	/mem'teɪn/	v.	保持,维持
attractive	/ə'træktɪv/	adj.	有吸引力的
preference	/'prefərəns/	n.	偏爱,优先选择
continuously	/kən'tɪnjuəsli/	adv.	连续地
premature	/ˌpremə'tʃʊə/	adj.	不成熟的,早产的,过早的
cancellation	/ˌkænsə'leɪʃən/	n.	取消,撤销
subject to			根据,依据;使承受
redeem	/rɪ'diːm/	vt.	赎回,偿还
redeemable	/rɪ'diːməbl/	adj.	可赎回的,可买回的
penalty	/'penlti/	n.	处罚,损失
prompt	/prɒmpt/	vt.	提示,指示

Exercise

I. Fill in the blank

1. A: Is there _____ I can do for you?
   B: I'd like to _____ _____ _____.
   A: 请问您需要什么帮助吗?
   B: 我想开个账户。

2. Our Great Wall _____ Card is completely suitable for you. It can be used for _____ _____ or _____ in any Bank of China branches all over China.
   我们有一种"长城电子借记卡",非常适合您的需求,它可以在全国范围内存款、取款。

3. You can _____ _____ _____ _____ at any of our branches. All transaction items of your card can be _____ on this book.
   您可以到北京中行任一网点来随时更新存折记录,您卡上的每一笔交易都会在存折上反映出来。

Deposit and Withdrawal Service

4. A: _____ do I need to deposit my money in your bank before I can withdraw it?

   B: The fixed deposit terms for _____ _____ are: one month, three months, six months, one year and two years. You can choose anyone of them.

   A: 存款在账户中储存多久才可以取？

   B: 外币定期存款的存款期限一共有 1 个月、3 个月、6 个月、一年、两年五个档次。您可以从中选择。

5. _____ _____ the term, _____ _____ the interest rate.

   定期存款存期越长利率越高。

6. The interest rate for _____ _____ is much higher than that of the savings account.

   定期存款的利息比活期储蓄存款的利率要高得多。

7. A: Ms. Smith, USD 1,000 has _____ _____ to your account. How do you want to deal with it?

   B: I need only USD 200 at present. And I'd like to deposit the rest to savings account.

   A: 史密斯女士，您的 1000 美元汇款已经汇到了，您打算怎么处理？

   B: 我目前只需要 200 美元现金，其余的我想存入储蓄帐户。

8. Please _____ your name on the remittance receipt.

   请先在这份汇款单上签字确认。

II. Translation

1. 请您核对一下存款凭证上打印的金额。

   _____

2. 定期存款能够提前支取吗？

   _____

3. 我要把活期存折上的人民币存成定期存单。

   _____

4. 如果您忘记密码的话，那只能办理密码挂失手续。

   _____

5. 储蓄账户是不允许透支的。

   _____

第二部分 外币兑换

Part II Foreign Currency Exchange

银行英语
Banking English

外币兑换-1

外币兑换一般手续

史密斯先生在中国银行北京市分行办理外币兑换业务。

 M: 大堂经理　T: 柜员　C: 客户

M: 早上好,先生。
C: 早上好,这儿是中国银行北京市分行,对吗?
M: 是的,不错。这是中国银行北京市分行,请问您要办理什么业务?
C: 好的,谢谢。我想兑换一些美元,可是我不知道怎么办。你知道这可是我第一次到北京,是来观看奥运会的。
M: 是这样?真诚欢迎您光临我市观看奥运会。瞧,就在那边标有"外币兑换"的3号柜台办理。请跟我来。
C: 谢谢你。
M: 没关系。

T: 早上好!
C: 早上好!
T: 能为您做点什么吗?
C: 您能为我将一些美元兑换成人民币吗?
T: 当然可以。您想换多少美元?另外,请问您是否带了护照?
C: 是的,我有。我想换100美元。
T: 请您填写水单一式三份。
C: 好,但我不清楚该如何填写?

General Procedures for Foreign Currency Exchange

Unit 1

Mr. Smith is changing foreign currency at Bank of China Beijing Branch.

M: Duty Manager   T: Teller   C: Customer

M: Good morning, Sir.
C: Good morning. This is Bank of China Beijing Branch, isn't it?
M: Yes. This is Bank of China Beijing Branch. Can I help you?
C: Yes, thanks. I want to change some US dollars here but I don't know how to do it. You know this is the first time I've been here in your city. I am here watching the Olympic Games.
M: Really? Welcome to our city for the Olympic Games. Look, over there, Counter No. 3 is the place where you can have foreign currencies changed. Please follow me and I will show you.
C: Thank you.
M: You are welcome.

T: Good morning, Sir!
C: Good morning.
T: What can I do for you?
C: I would like to change some US dollars into Renminbi.
T: Certainly. How much would you like to change and do you have your passport?
C: Yes, I have and I want to change 100 US dollars.
T: Please fill out this exchange memo in **triplicate**.
C: OK, but how do I fill it out?

> **exchange** /ɪksˈtʃeɪndʒ/ vt. 交换，兑换，交流，交易
> **triplicate** /ˈtrɪplɪkɪt/ adj. 三倍的，三重的

Banking English

T: 水单一式三份,请您将姓名、地址和电话填在这里,兑换金额填在这里,然后在下面签字。其余都由我来帮您填写。

C: 好的,顺便问一下,今天的美元现钞价是多少?

T: 让我帮您查一下……100 美元兑换人民币 757.00。

C: 那么,您能给我解释一下买价和卖价的区别吗?

T: 当然可以。以美元为例,银行卖出美元时,使用卖出价,从您手中买入美元时,用买入价。也就是说,"买"和"卖"是从银行的角度定义的。

C: 明白了,这是钞票和水单。

T: 我可以看一下您的护照吗?

C: 对了,这是我的护照。

T: 好了,史密斯先生。这是您的钱、护照和水单。

C: 没错,非常感谢!

T: 不客气,顺便提一句,请保存好水单。将来您或许会用得着。

C: 为什么这么说呢?

T: 如果您想把未用完的人民币兑回外币,您需要向银行出示这份水单。

C: 我明白了,谢谢您,再见!

T: 再见!

NOTES

1. in triplicate 一式三份 类似的还有 duplicate 两份,quadruplicate 四份 相当于 in two, three and four copies

2. buying rate 买价 分为现钞买入价:buying rate for foreign cash/bank notes 和现汇买入价:buying rate for foreign exchange 而卖价则是 selling rate 这里买卖价都是从银行角度讲的 from the bank's point of view

3. by the way 顺便问一下

Foreign Currency Exchange

T: The exchange memo is in triplicate. Please write your name, your address and your telephone number here and the amount here. Also, please sign at the bottom. I'll fill out the rest for you.

C: OK. By the way, what's today's rate for US dollar notes?

T: Let me check it for you... It's 757.00 Yuan for 100 US dollars.

C: Could you tell me the difference between the buying rate and the selling rate?

T: Sure. Take the US dollars for example. When we sell US dollars to you, the selling rate is applied. Whereas when we buy US dollars from you, the buying rate is used. That is to say, the "buying rate" and "selling rate" are defined from the bank's point of view.

C: I see. Here are the notes and the memo.

T: And your passport please?

C: Oh, yes. Here you are.

T: Well, Mr. Smith. Here you are... your money, your passport and the memo.

C: Correct. Thank you very much.

T: You are welcome. By the way, please hold on to the memo. You may find it useful in the future.

C: Why?

T: With this exchange memo you will be able to exchange the unused RMB back into US dollars.

C: I see. Thanks a lot. Good bye!

T: Good bye!

define /dɪ'faɪn/ vt. 定义，详细说明

银行英语
Banking English

外币兑换-2

保管兑换水单

史密斯先生在中国银行北京市分行把欧元兑换成人民币,柜员请他注意保管兑换水单。

 M: 大堂经理　T: 柜员　C: 客户

M: 下午好,史密斯先生,真高兴又见到您,您今天看来非常高兴。
C: 您好。我昨天观看了北京奥运会开幕式,太精彩了。中国了不起。北京太好了。
M: 谢谢。祝贺您观看了北京奥运会开幕式,感谢您对中国的赞美。您今天还需要什么帮助吗?
C: 我想在中国各地多走走,多看看。还要兑换一些外币。
M: 太好了。欢迎您在我国多看看。请您到3号柜台办理业务。
T: 下午好!
C: 下午好!
T: 我可以帮您吗?
C: 我想兑换点钱。
T: 好的,您想兑换什么货币?
C: 500欧元。
T: 好吧,请您填写兑换水单一式三份好吗?
C: 太感谢了。喏,水单、我的护照,还有500欧元。

Foreign Currency Exchange

Keeping the Exchange Memo

Mr. Smith is changing some Euros into RMB at Bank of China Beijing Branch. The bank clerk asks him to keep the exchange memo.

M: Duty Manager T: Teller C: Customer

M: Good afternoon, Mr. Smith. I am very glad to see you again. You look so happy today.

C: Good afternoon. I watched the opening ceremony of the Beijing Olympic Games yesterday. It was fantastic. China is great, Beijing is great.

M: Thank you very much. I am glad that you went to the opening ceremony, and I am also thankful for your compliment of our country. What can I do for you today?

C: I am thinking of visiting other cities too, so I need to have some more cash changed into RMB.

M: That is fine. We are happy to assist you. Please go to Counter No. 3.

T: Good afternoon!

C: Good afternoon!

T: May I help you?

C: I want to change some money.

T: What money do you wish to change?

C: 500 Euros.

T: Would you please fill out this exchange memo in triplicate?

C: It is very kind of you. Here you are... the memo, my passport and 500 Euros.

> Euro /ˈjuərəu/ *n.* 欧元

Banking English

T: 谢谢。今天，欧元对人民币的汇率是 972.16，500 欧元兑人民币 4860.80 元。好了，这是您的钱、护照和水单。请保存好水单，将来也许会用得着。
C: 为什么？
T: 如果您想把未用完的人民币兑回外币，就要向银行出示这份水单。
C: 非常感谢，再见！
T: 不客气，再见！

NOTES

1. exchange memo 兑换水单
2. 在谈论汇率的时候，对于同样一句中文，我们可以用许多方式表达。这些表达虽然大同小异，有些甚至不是很规范，但却在实际运用中较为有效，例如当我们想说"美元兑人民币汇率为 799.23"时，我们可以说：

   (1) It's 799.23 Yuan for 100 US dollars.
   (2) It's RMB 799.23 against 100 US dollars.
   (3) It's RMB 799.23 per 100 US dollars.
   (4) The exchange rate today is "seven-nine-nine-point-two-three".

外币兑换
Foreign Currency Exchange

T: Thank you. Our buying rate for notes today is 972.16 RMB per 100 Euros and your total will be 4860.80 Yuan for 500 Euros. Now, here is your money, your passport and the memo. Please don't lose the memo. You may find it useful later.

C: Why?

T: You have to show the memo to the bank when you convert any unused RMB back into Euros.

C: Thanks a lot. Good-bye!

T: You are welcome. Good-bye!

note /nəʊt/ *n.* 票据, 纸币
convert /kən'vət/ *vt.* 转换

中国银行股份有限公司北京怀柔支行
Bank of China Limited Beijing Huairou Subbranch

外币兑换—3

收取手续费规定

一位在机场工作的柜员正在向外国客户解释银行收取兑换手续费的标准问题。

T: 柜员　　C: 客户

T: 您好,先生,请问您要办理什么业务?
C: 你好,请问可以把我的外币换成人民币吗?
T: 请问您用什么货币换?
C: 有一些美元,还有一些澳元。
T: 可以,这些钱分别有多少呢?
C: 让我看看,澳元有500多,美元有200多。
T: 先生,根据规定,对于单笔交易金额小于等值500美元的外币现钞兑入,我们是要收取每笔30元的手续费的,可以么?
C: 那么其他银行有这种手续费吗?
T: 这个问题我们不太确定,各行的规定不一样。
C: 好的,那你帮我换一下吧。
T: 好,这是您的人民币、回单、手续费收据。
C: 谢谢,哎,我的钱不是超过500美元了吗?为什么收我60元钱?

Foreign Currency Exchange

The Charge Standard for Foreign Currency Exchange

Unit 3

A teller at the Airport is explaining to a foreign customer about the service charge regulations for foreign currency exchange.

T: Teller   C: Customer

T: Hello, Sir. What can I do for you?
C: Hi, can you exchange my money into RMB?
T: Sure, which currency would you like to exchange?
C: Some US dollars and some Australian dollars.
T: OK. How much of each?
C: Oh, let me see. I have more than five hundred Australian dollars and more than two hundred US dollars.
T: Sir, according to our regulations, there will be a 30 yuan RMB service charge for each exchange that is less than five hundred US dollars or its equivalent of foreign currency. Is that OK with you?
C: Other banks charge the same, don't they?
T: Sorry, we are not sure about that. Different banks have different charge policies.
C: OK, please go ahead.
T: Sir, here is your RMB. This is your memo, and this is your receipt for the service charge.
C: Thank you! Hey, I changed more than 500 dollars, why were you charging me 60 yuan?

equivalent /ɪˈkwɪvələnt/ n. 同等, 等同物
receipt /rɪˈsiːt/ n. 收条, 收据; 收到

银行英语
Banking English

T: 先生，我们收费的标准是单笔交易不足500美元收取30元手续费，因为您给我们的是两种货币而且都不足500美元，在我们的系统中，是作为两笔交易收取的。

C: 好吧，谢谢。再见。

T: 再见。欢迎您的再次光临。

NOTES

1. according to 依照，根据
2. service charge 手续费，也可以理解为服务费，相似的表达还有 handling charge
3. more than 多于
   less than 少于
4. regulation 监管规定，银行内部政策为 bank policy

中国银行股份有限公司北京顺义支行
Bank of China Limited Beijing Shunyi Subbranch

Foreign Currency Exchange

T: Sir, our service charge policy is 30 RMB for each money exchange transaction less than 500 US dollars. You gave me two different kinds of currencies, and they are both less than 500 US dollars. So our computer system takes it as two separate transactions.

C: OK. Thank you! Bye.

T: Bye. Please come back.

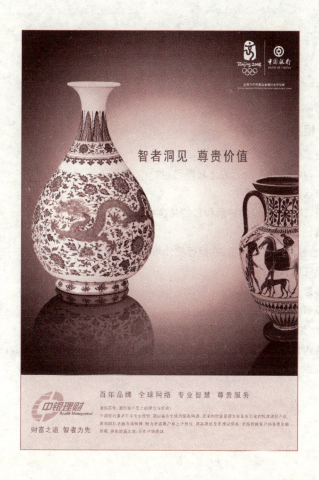

银行英语
Banking English

外币兑换—4

非居民兑换外币

> 我们国家对于居民与非居民购买外汇设定了非常严格的管理规定。一位外国客户不久就会离开中国，回到自己的家乡去。现在，他希望将在中国的人民币收入兑换成他本国的货币。那么，银行柜员都会让这位外国客户提供什么证明材料呢？

T: 柜员　　C: 客户

T: 先生您好，请问您要办理什么业务？
C: 您好，我是 AAA 公司的外籍顾问，我马上要回国，可不可以把手中的人民币换成我自己国家的货币呢？
T: 当然，请您出示您的护照和您的兑换水单。
C: 什么？水单？
T: 对，也就是您当初入境，在银行把外币兑换成人民币时银行给您的兑换证明。
C: 兑换证明，我没有。
T: 那么您有用外卡取现的证明么？
C: 也没有。
T: 先生，请问您的这些人民币是通过何种途径得到的？
C: 这些人民币是 AAA 公司支付给我的顾问费，一共是 7000 元，怎么，有问题么？

Foreign Currency Exchange

Non-Residents Purchasing Foreign Currency

The State Administration of Foreign Exchange (SAFE) has very strict regulations about residents and non-residents alike purchasing foreign currencies in China. A foreigner is leaving China for his own country. Now he would like to convert his RMB income in China into his home currency. What documents or certificates will the bank clerk ask the foreign customer to provide?

T: Teller   C: Customer

T: Good morning, Sir, what can I do for you?

C: Good morning, I am an advisor in AAA Co, Ltd., and I am about to go back to my country. I wonder if I could change these RMB into the currency of my own country.

T: Certainly, please show me your passport and the exchange memo.

C: What? The exchange memo?

T: Yes, it is the certificate proving that you exchanged your country's currency into RMB when you first came to China.

C: Sorry, but I don't have that kind of certificate.

T: Then, do you have any certificate showing you use your credit card from your own country, to withdraw RMB cash in China?

C: I don't have that either.

T: Sir, could you tell me how you got these RMB?

C: They are my advisory fees paid by AAA Co, Ltd. And the total amount is 7,000 Yuan. Is there anything wrong?

Banking English

T: 没有问题,是这样的,根据我们国家的规定,像您这种情况,您需要提供护照、您的工作合同、完税证明、收入证明这几项证明的原件和复印件,我们会根据这些资料为您办理批汇业务,把您的人民币兑换为外币。您看可以吗?

C: 这么麻烦,没有别的办法吗?

T: 对不起,先生,按照外汇管理规定,入境后兑换的人民币,到离境时没有用完的,我行可以凭当时的兑换水单作为证明为您办理退汇业务,除此之外,像您在中国境内取得的收入,必须提供刚才所说的资料,才能为您办理批汇业务进行兑换。

C: 好吧,让我来找一找……这些可以么?

T: 可以,请您填写一下这张表格,并且稍等一下,马上为您办理兑换手续。

C: 好,给您。

T: 给您。这是美元现金,还有证件。

C: 谢谢!

T: 不客气,再见!

C: 再见!

NOTES

1. tax completion certificate 完税证明,也可用 tax payment certificate 或 duty-paid certificate 表达
2. the foreign exchange administration 外汇管理 the State Administration of Foreign Exchange(SAFE) 是指国家外汇管理局
3. employment contract 工作合同
4. labor contract 劳动合同
5. option 可选择的范围,也作 alternative

Foreign Currency Exchange

T: No. But according to the regulations of the State Administration of Foreign Exchange, we need a couple of things to do the money exchange for you. To be specific, we need your passport, your employment contract, your income certificate and relevant tax completion certificate.

C: That's too complicated. Is there any other way?

T: Sorry, Sir, the options are quite limited. That is why I asked you about the exchange memo just now. When you first came to our country, you must have changed some foreign currency into RMB. At that time, we gave you the exchange memo, with which you can change the unused RMB back into the foreign currency when you leave China. Apart from that, any RMB income you earned in our country is not allowed for exchange unless you can present the documents I mentioned before.

C: OK, then let me have a look... Is this all right?

T: Yes, that is the exchange memo we want. Please fill out this form, and wait a moment. I will exchange your money as soon as possible.

C: OK. Here you are.

T: Right, here is the US dollar cash and your passport.

C: Thanks!

T: You are welcome. Good-bye.

C: Bye.

银行英语
Banking English

外币兑换—5

外币兑换二例

罗伯特先生在中国银行向大堂经理询问何种外币可以在中国兑换成人民币。

T: 柜员   C: 客户

- C: 你好,你这里兑换外币吗?
- M: 是的,我可以为您做点什么?
- C: 我是想问问你们可以兑换什么货币?
- M: 我们可以兑换美元、英镑、欧元、日元、港币等17种货币。
- C: 卢布呢?
- M: 我们目前不办理卢布兑换。
- C: 卢比呢?
- M: 也不办理。
- C: 为什么?
- M: 这是我国中央银行的规定。
- C: 谢谢!
- M: 不客气,再见。

Foreign Currency Exchange

Two Examples of Foreign Currency Exchange

Robert is asking the duty manager at Bank of China about what kinds of foreign currencies could be changed into RMB in China.

T: Teller   C: Customer

C: Good afternoon, can I change some money in your bank?

M: Yes, I think I can help you with that.

C: I'd like to know what kinds of foreign currencies I can change in your bank.

M: We can change US dollars, the Pound sterling, Euros, Japanese yen, Hong Kong dollars, etc. Altogether there are 17 kinds of foreign currencies.

C: How about Ruble?

M: Sorry, we don't change Rubles at present.

C: How about Rupee?

M: No, we don't change those either.

C: Why?

M: That is the foreign currency policy of our central bank.

C: Thank you.

M: You are welcome. Goodbye.

---

etc. /et'setərə/ 等等, 是 et cetera 的缩写

Ruble /'ru:bəl/ n. 卢布(俄罗斯货币单位)

Rupee /'ru:pi:/ n. 卢比(印度等的货币单位)

银行英语
Banking English

罗伯特先生明天就要回美国了。他希望将手中的日元兑换成美元,这就是所谓的个人实盘外汇买卖业务了。

T: 柜员　C: 客户

T: 您好。您需要什么帮助吗?

C: 您好!我准备明天启程去美国,在到达那里时,我需要随身带些美元,我能在这里用日元买到美元吗?

T: 可以,先生。您想买多少?

C: 哦,我想要100美元左右。前几天我已经办理了旅行支票,但是,我不想在到达美国时手头没有现金。机场非常拥挤的时候,兑现旅行支票是件很麻烦的事。

T: 的确是这样。请您填写一下外汇买卖申请表。

C: 好。

T: 这是给您的现金和兑换单。

C: 谢谢!再见!

NOTES

1. 目前我行可以收兑的外币币种包括:

   Pound sterling 英镑　Hong Kong dollar 港币　American/U.S. dollar 美元
   Swiss Franc 瑞士法郎　Macao Pataca 澳门元
   Danish Krone(复数:Kronur)丹麦克朗
   Norwegian Krone(复数:Kronur)挪威克朗
   Swedish Krona(复数:Kronor)瑞典克朗
   Japanese yen 日元　Canadian dollar 加拿大元　Australian Dollar 澳大利亚元
   Euro 欧元　Korea Won 韩元　Philippine Peso 菲律宾比索　Thailand Baht 泰国铢

2. the central bank 意指中央银行,在我国即指中国人民银行,但向外国客户解释起来可能比较麻烦,所以可以在用到中国人民银行时用中央银行来表达。我国的银行业监管机构为银监会(China Banking Supervisory Commission,缩编为CBRC)。

3. leave for 指出发前往,需要注意的是"leave for"后面应该接去往的目的地。

4. change Japanese yen into US dollars,指用日元买美元,想要较口语化一些,我们还可以说"buy some US dollars with Japanese yen"等。在柜台使用时可以灵活使用,不必拘泥于某一种表达方式,只要把意思表达清楚即可。

Foreign Currency Exchange

Robert is leaving for America tomorrow. He wants to change some Japanese yen into U.S. dollars. That is the "Personal foreign exchange trading business".

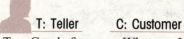

T: Teller   C: Customer

T: Good afternoon. What can I do for you?

C: Good afternoon, I'm leaving for America tomorrow. I need to have some US dollars with me when I arrive there. Can I change some Japanese yen into US dollars in your bank?

T: Certainly, Sir. How much would you like to buy?

C: Well, I'd like to buy about one hundred dollars. I bought some travelers' cheques several days ago. But I don't want to arrive in America without cash. You know, it's crazy to cash traveler's cheques when the airport is very crowded.

T: Exactly, now please fill out the application form of foreign currency trading business.

C: OK.

T: Here is your cash and exchange receipt.

C: Thank you! Goodbye!

arrive /əˈraɪv/ vi. 到达，抵达
crowded /ˈkraʊdɪd/ adj. 拥挤的

Banking English

外币兑换 —6

解释为何没收假钞

史密斯先生来银行兑换美元，柜员在其中发现两张假钞。

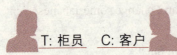

T: 柜员　　C: 客户

T: 您需要帮忙吗？
C: 是的，我想兑换点美钞，给，一共500美元。
T: 请您填写一下兑换水单，并出示您的护照。
C: 给。
T: 请稍候。对不起，史密斯先生，我们发现这两张百元面额的美钞是伪造的。
C: 是吗？这怎么可能呢？这样吧，你把它们还给我。
T: 对不起，史密斯先生，按照我国中央银行的规定，假钞应予以没收，所以我们不能把它还给您。我们可以给您一张没收收据。
C: 我不想要什么收据，也不想兑换了，请把我的钱都还给我，这事就了结了。
T: 很抱歉，史密斯先生，我只能把其余三张钞票还给您，根据我国中央银行的规定，银行发现假钞必须没收。
C: 好吧，也许你是对的，那我也只好兑换其他三张了。
T: 谢谢合作，这是没收收据，还有人民币，给您。
C: 谢谢！

NOTES

1. forged/counterfeit/fake note 假钞

   e.g. The counterfeit note must be confiscated once it is found. 发现假钞必须予以没收。

2. certificate of confiscation 没收收据

Explanations about Confiscating Counterfeit Note

Mr. Smith comes to change some US dollars, but the clerk finds two counterfeit notes among them.

T: Teller   C: Customer

T: Can I help you?
C: Yes, I'd like to change some US dollars, here you are, 500 dollars.
T: Please fill in this exchange memo and show me your passport.
C: OK, here it is.
T: Wait a moment please. Excuse me, Mr. Smith, we found these two hundred US dollar notes are counterfeit.
C: Are they? How can that be? Then give them back to me.
T: Sorry, Mr. Smith, according to the regulations of our country's central bank, forged notes must be confiscated. We can't give them back to you. Instead, we'll give you a certificate of confiscation.
C: I don't want to change the money and I don't need any of your certificates. Just give me my money, and then it's over. Nothing has happened.
T: I'm very sorry, Mr. Smith. I can only return the other three US dollar notes to you because the bank must confiscate forged notes once they are found according to our central bank's regulations.
C: OK, maybe you're right. Just change the other three notes for me.
T: Thank you for your cooperation. This is the certificate of confiscation and the RMB. Here you are.
C: Thank you!

counterfeit /'kaʊntəfit/ adj. 伪造的, 假的　　n. 伪造物, 假钞
regulation /ˌrejʊ'leɪʃən/ n. 规则, 规章
forge /fɔːdʒ/ vt. 锻造, 伪造
confiscate /'kɒnfɪskeɪt/ vt. 没收
confiscation /ˌkɒnfɪs'keɪʃən/ n. 没收

Banking English

外币兑换—7

介绍假币的一般特征和没收假币的手续

一位外籍人很快要回国了,到银行来办理退汇,却被发现其中有一张钱是假钞。

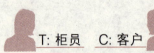

T: 柜员   C: 客户

T: 您好,请问您办理什么业务?
C: 我前几天在中国银行用美元兑换了一些人民币,现在要回国了,想把没有用完的人民币换回美元。这里可以办理退汇业务吗?
T: 当然可以。请出示您的护照和上次兑换人民币时银行给您的兑换水单。
C: 给您。
T: 请稍等……对不起,您给我的人民币里有一张50元的假币。
C: 哦,真的吗?
T: 没错!的确是假币。
C: 可我怎么知道这张钱是假币呢?
T: 我给您拿一张真币,两个对照着看一下您就明白了。您看:这张假币的水印特别模糊,而真币的水印很清晰而且有立体感;假币的防伪线是印刷上去的,而真币防伪线是独立的,可用针挑出来;假币盲文的圆点没有凹凸感,而真币的凹凸感

Foreign Currency Exchange

General Features of Counterfeit Notes and Confiscation Procedures

Unit 7

A foreigner is going back home soon and he comes into a bank to re-exchange unused RMB. Unfortunately, there is one fake note in the money he brings.

T: Teller   C: Customer

T: Hello, what can I do for you?

C: I changed some US dollars to RMB several days ago in Bank of China. Now I am going back to my own country and I'd like to convert the remaining RMB back to US Dollars. Can I do it here?

T: Certainly. Please show me your passport and the exchange memo the bank gave you when you changed money last time.

C: Here you are.

T: Please wait a moment... Excuse me, Sir. There is one forged note of 50 Yuan in the money you gave me.

C: Oh, really?

T: Yes. I am afraid that it is indeed a forged one.

C: But how do I know it is a fake! Why is it fake?

T: OK. I will show you a real note. You just compare the two and then you will see the differences: Here, the watermark of the forged note is indistinct while the real one is clear and three-dimensional; the security line of the counterfeit note is printed on while that of the real one is metallic and independent; the Braille dots have no feeling of concave-convex on the fake one, while the real one has a raised feeling; the false one has

change /tʃemdʒ/ v. 兑换
watermark /'wɔːtəmɑːk/ n. 水印
indistinct /ˌindis'tiŋkt/ adj. 模糊的, 不清楚的
three-dimensional /θriː-dɪ'menʃənəl/ adj. 立体感, 三维的
independent /indi'pendənt/ adj. 独立的
dot /dɒt/ n. 圆点

Banking English

很明显;假币在紫光灯下没有荧光反映,而真币可以看到"50"的荧光字样。另外,这张假币的纸质又薄又脆,而真币很有柔韧性。

C: 哎……看来这真是张假币。那我给你换一张真的吧,我想把这张假币留作纪念。

T: 对不起,根据我国中央银行的规定,各家银行发现假币必须没收。这是没收假币收据,请您在收据上签名。

C: 好吧。

T: 谢谢您。请您收好收据,这上面有那张假币的编号,您如有疑问可以到上级主管部门再次鉴定。这是办理退汇给您退还的美元,请您收好。

C: 谢谢。

NOTES

1. 纸币主要的防伪特征:

    security line 安全线   fiber threads 纤维丝   watermarks 水印
    magnetic ink 磁性油墨   fluorescent ink 变色油墨

2. feeling of concave-convex 凹凸感

中国银行股份有限公司北京芳星园支行
Bank of China Limited Beijing Fangxingyuan Subbranch

Foreign Currency Exchange

no reflection under the fluorescent lamp while the real one's fluorescent ink has. Also, the paper of the forged note is flimsy while the real one is pliable and strong.

C: Wow, it looks like it really is a forged note. Can I keep that forged one as a souvenir? I will give you a real one instead.

T: Sorry, according to the regulations of our country's central bank, every bank should confiscate forged notes once they are found. This is the certificate of confiscation. Please sign your name on it.

C: All right.

T: Thank you. Please keep the certificate which has the serial number of the forged note on it. If you have any doubt about the note we confiscate, you can contact the central bank of our country to re-authenticate it. Here are the US dollars exchanged for you. Please have a cheque.

C: Thank you.

authenticate /ɔːˈθentɪkeɪt/ v. 鉴定
reflection /rɪˈflekʃən/ adj. 反射,反照
fluorescent /ˈfluəˈresənt/ adj. 荧光
flimsy /ˈflɪmzɪ/ adj. 轻而薄的;脆弱的

Banking English

补充单词

duplicate	/'djuːplikeɪt/	adj.	复制的,副的,两重的
quadruplicate	/kwɒ'druːplɪkɪt/	adj.	四倍的
pleasure	/'pleʒə/	n.	愉快,快乐
prescript	/'priːskrɪpt/	n.	指示,规定
exactly	/ɪg'zæktli/	adv.	正确地
braille	/breɪl/	n.	盲文
breakable	/'breɪkəbəl/	adj.	易碎的

Exercise

I. Fill in the blank

1. Please _____ _____ this form first.
   请先填写一下这份表格。

2. Please copy your passport in _____.
   请把您的护照复印一式三份。

3. I want to _____ foreign money into RMB.
   我想把外币兑成人民币。

4. What is the _____ _____ today for US dollar against RMB?
   请问今天美元兑人民币的汇率是多少?

5. _____ the weather report, we shall have cold weather next week.
   根据天预报,我们下周会迎来寒冷天气。

6. I'll _____ Shanghai _____ Beijing.
   我将离开上海前往北京。

7. I would like to _____ some traveler's cheques.
   我想兑一些旅行支票。

8. According to the regulations, the _____ must be _____.
   根据规定,假钞必须被没收。

9. Please _____ the _____ with the real one.
   请将假钞和真钞做个比较。

10. There is no feeling of _____ of the Braille on the _____ while the real one has a strong raised feeling.
    假钞上的盲文没有凹凸感而真钞感觉明显。

Foreign Currency Exchange

11. If you have any doubt, you could contact the central bank to _____ it.
    如果有疑议,您可以到我们的上级部门去做再次鉴定。
12. Could you _____ me your _____ please?
    请出示您的护照好吗?
13. Could you tell me what is the _____ of USD now please?
    请您告诉我现在美元的卖出价好吗?

中国银行股份有限公司北京首都机场支行
Bank of China Limited Beijing Capital Airport Subbranch

第三部分 旅行支票
Part III Traveler's Cheques

银行英语
Banking English

旅行支票—1

咨询旅行支票托收

中国银行某支行网点柜台，史密斯先生的旅行支票由于背书栏没有按规定填写而无法直接兑付，在银行职员的建议下他办理了支票托收。

 T: 柜员　　 C: 客户

T: 您好，请问您需要什么帮助吗？
C: 你好，我想兑现这张100美元的支票。
T: 对不起，您的支票背书栏上填写了支票的面额，这属于不合格支票，我们无法直接为您兑现。
C: 是不是就作废了呢？
T: 您可以申请办理托收。
C: 那我应该怎么做呢？
T: 好的，请您填写一下支票托收申请表。
C: 需要多少天能收到钱？
T: 大约40天，到时我们会通知您，您需要携带护照、申请表前来办理取款手续。
C: 为什么要这么多天？

中国银行股份有限公司北京东城支行
Bank of China Limited Beijing Dongcheng Subbranch

Inquiring about Traveler's Cheques Collection

At a counter of one sub-branch of Bank of China, Mr. Smith wants to cash his traveler's cheque. But his cheque has been endorsed incorrectly and cannot be accepted by the bank. A bank clerk thus suggests that he have his cheque collected.

T: Teller   C: Customer

T: Hello, what can I do for you?
C: Hello, I'd like to cash my 100 US dollars traveler's cheque.
T: OK. Uh...I'm sorry that your cheque is mistakenly endorsed, you see, with the denomination written at the wrong place, which is unacceptable at our bank. I am afraid our bank can't cash it for you right away.
C: Are you telling me the cheque cannot be used anymore?
T: It's not that serious. You can place a request for cheque collection.
C: Then, what shall I do?
T: OK, please fill out the application form for cheque collection.
C: How many days do I have to wait to get my money back?
T: About 40 days... we will inform you by telephone as soon as we get the money back, and you should bring your passport and this application form back next time when you come to collect the money.
C: Why does it take so many days?

> cash /kæʃ/ n. 现金
>   vt. 兑现
> cheque /tʃek/ n. 支票,检讫的记号,饭馆的账单
> denomination /dɪˌnɒmɪˈneɪʃən/ n. (度量衡或货币)
>   类别或单位
> application form 申请表格

Banking English

T: 我们需要将您的支票寄往国外向有关清算行要求付款。在一定时期内,款项有被国外行收回的可能。所以,我行必须在确认款项无误后才能兑付给您。

C: 明白了,40 天后我可以委托别人来取款吗?

T: 当然可以,但是要带上委托人和您两个人的护照和托收申请书。

C: 今天我要交多少费用呢?

T: 手续费每笔折人民币按 1‰ 收取,最低 50 元,最高 250 元,邮费每笔 10 元。 您需要交 60 元人民币的手续费。

C: 谢谢,你真是帮了我大忙了!

T: 别客气。欢迎您再次到我行办理业务。再见!

C: 再见!

NOTES

1. cash *n.* 现金 *vt.* 兑现

   e.g. Excuse me, but I've no cash on me. 对不起,我身边没带现钱。

   e.g. Can you cash this traveler's cheque for me now?
   你现在能帮我兑现这张旅行支票吗?

2. cheque/cheque *n.* 支票;检讫的记号;饭馆的账单

   e.g. Can I pay it by cheque? 我能不能用支票支付?

   美式英语中,cheque 又作"钞票"解释,相当于英式英语中的 banknote。

3. entrust(委托)的用法:entrust sb. with sth. 或者 entrust sth. to sb.

   e.g. He entrusted his aides with the task./ He entrusted the task to his aides.
   他把这项任务委托给了他的助手们。

4. charge *v.* 收费 *n.* 费用

   柜台服务中经常用到的短语有:handling charge 手续费   service charge 服务费   cash withdrawal charge 取现费   ...to be charged 需要收费

Traveler's Cheques

T: We have to send the cheque by post to the drawer bank abroad and

entrust /ɪnˈtrʌst/ v. 委托
handle /ˈhændl/ v. 触摸；买卖；处理，操作

ask the relative clearing bank for the repayment. But there is the possibility that the relative clearing bank may dishonor the cheque or delay repayment. So, we have to wait until we actually receive the money.

C: Oh I see. Can I entrust somebody else to withdraw the money after forty days?

T: Of course, but the passports for both of you and the application form are required.

C: How much do you charge for this service?

T: The commission is 1‰ of the total amount of the cheques that you want to collect and it is paid in RMB according to the exchange rate today, 50 Yuan minimum and 250 Yuan maximum. Plus, the postage is 10 Yuan. So, let me see... altogether you need to pay a 60 Yuan handling charge.

C: Thank you very much. You are very helpful!

T: My pleasure. Welcome to our bank anytime.

C: Goodbye!

银行英语
Banking English

旅行支票—2

复签、贴息及买卖差价

玛丽小姐想在银行办理旅行支票的兑付业务,柜台人员热情地接待了她。

T: 柜员　　C: 客户

T: 您好。请问办理什么业务?
C: 您好,我想兑付旅行支票。
T: 需要出示您的护照及旅行支票。
C: 好的。我想兑付5400美元的旅支。
T: 请出示一下您的购买协议。
C: 为什么?
T: 按规定如果兑换金额大于5000美元,需要出示您的购买协议。
C: 好的,这是我的购买协议。
T: 谢谢。请您在旅行支票上复签,并填写兑换水单。
C: 没问题。
T: 您是想兑换成美元还是人民币?
C: 手续费不一样吗?
T: 不一样。无论您兑换成人民币还是美元,都需要扣除0.75%的贴息,兑换美元还需另扣买卖差价。
C: 为什么要收贴息及买卖差价?

Traveler's Cheques

Countersignature, Discount and Cash Withdrawal Charge

Unit 2

Ms. Martin wants to cash some traveler's cheques in the bank. The bank clerk helps her with the business enthusiastically.

T: Teller   C: Customer

T: Hello, Madam! How can I help you?
C: Hello, can I cash some traveler's cheques here?
T: Of course, would you please give me your passport and the traveler's cheques?
C: Well, I need to cash 5,400 US dollars in traveler's cheques.
T: Would you please show me your purchase agreement?
C: Why?
T: According to our regulations if the total amount you want to cash is more than 5,000 US dollars, you'll have to present your purchase agreement.
C: OK, this is my purchase agreement.
T: Thank you. Then would you please countersign them here and fill out this exchange memo?
C: No problem.
T: Would you like to have US dollars or RMB?
C: The charge is the same, isn't it?
T: Well, no, I'm afraid. First, so long as you cash your traveler's cheques, whether you want RMB or US dollars, there is a discount of 0.75%. And second, if you want US dollars cash, there's another cash withdrawal charge of around 0.3%.
C: Why is there such a discount and why do I have to pay for drawing my own money?

countersign /ˈkaʊntəsaɪn/ v. 复签, 会签, 副署, 连署
discount /ˈdɪskaʊnt/ n. 贴息, 贴现, 折扣

T: 因为您的旅行支票是由国外旅行支票公司发行的,我们要将您的旅行支票寄往代理机构去清算,我们需支付保险费和运费,并且需要等一段时间才能被偿还,但我们已经把钱垫付给您,0.75%就是这段时间垫付款的费用。而买卖差价则是由于旅行支票属于汇户,根据国家规定境外个人从汇户里取现金需要收取一定的差价。

C: 我明白了。请帮我兑付500美元的现金,剩下的要人民币。

T: 好的,请稍等。……这是您的500美元,这是人民币、您的护照、水单,请您核对。

C: 非常正确,谢谢你的解释及服务。

T: 您太客气了。请走好。

C: 再见!

T: 再见!

NOTES

1. "I'm afraid..." 在日常柜台服务中,受到规章制度的约束或是因为软硬件条件所限,并不是客户提出的所有请求我们都可以满足。这些时候,使用 "I'm afraid..." (很抱歉,恐怕……) 就是一种比较礼貌地表达拒绝的方法。例如:

   e.g. I am afraid that we can only exchange 500 US dollars for you today.
   　　很抱歉,我今天只能为您兑换500美元。

   e.g. I am afraid that I couldn't go with you to the ball tonight.
   　　对不起,恐怕今晚我不能和你一起去舞会了。

2. appreciate v. 赏识,鉴赏,感激

   e.g. I appreciate you very much. 我非常欣赏/感谢你。

   e.g. It is greatly appreciated.=Thank you very much. 非常感谢。

3. passport 指护照。Please show me your passport. 请出示您的护照。
   passbook 存折。update the passbook 登折 password 密码
   key in the password 输入密码

旅行支票
Traveler's Cheques

T: Well, as your cheques are issued by a foreign traveler's cheques company, our bank has to send these

> reimbursement /ˌriːɪmˈbɜːsmənt/ n. 偿还，退还
> category /ˈkætɪɡəri/ n. 类型
> appreciate /əˈpriːʃieɪt/ v. 赏识，鉴赏，感激

cheques back to the company or its agency to get reimbursement. We have to pay the insurance and the freight in the whole process and it takes time. But before that, you've already got your cash from the bank, which means the bank offers a loan to you. That 0.75% discount, therefore, can be regarded as the interest of advance payment of the bank. As for the cash withdrawal charge, according to relevant regulations by China's State Administration of Foreign Exchange, your traveler's cheques fall into the category of foreign exchange account, and thus any foreign currency cash withdrawal from the account is to be charged.

C: I see. Please give me 500 US dollars cash and the rest all in RMB.

T: OK, please wait a moment... Here is your 500 US dollars, and here is the RMB, your passport and the exchange memo. Please check it yourself.

C: Excellent! I really appreciate your help.

T: You are welcome. Have a good time in Beijing.

C: See you!

T: See you!

银行英语
Banking English

旅行支票—3

当面复签及不可代兑旅支

某外国客户正在向银行的工作人员咨询有关旅行支票的复签和兑付事宜。

T：柜员　　C：客户

- T： 您好！欢迎光临。
- C： 您好，我想兑付600美元的旅行支票换成人民币。
- T： 请出示您的护照及旅行支票。
- C： 好的。
- T： 对不起，您的复签已经签过了，麻烦您在旅行支票的背面再重新签一次。
- C： 为什么？这是我的护照，你可以核对护照上的签字。
- T： 很抱歉，按照国际惯例，您必须在银行柜台进行复签。
- C： 好吧。
- C： 我还有一张旅行支票是我朋友的，我可以替他兑现吗？他现在在医院。
- T： 很抱歉，旅行支票必须本人持护照来银行才可以兑现，希望您可以理解。

中国银行股份有限公司北京长安支行
Bank of China Limited Beijing Chang'an Subbranch

Countersigning in the Presence of the Bank Clerk and Cashing in Person

A foreign guest is asking the bank clerk about countersigning and cashing traveler's cheques.

T: Teller   C: Customer

T: Hello! Is there anything I can do for you?

C: Yes, I would like to change my 600 US dollars traveler's cheques into RMB.

T: OK, would you please give me your passport and the traveler's cheques?

C: Sure, here they are.

T: Sorry, Sir, your cheques have already been countersigned. Would you please countersign them again at the back of the cheques?

C: Why do I have to do it? You see, this is my passport with my photo and my signature on it, too. You can just compare my signature on the cheques with that on my passport.

T: Well, sir, I am sorry for the inconvenience. But according to international common practice, you must countersign the cheques in the presence of the bank clerk.

C: OK, then ...I'll do it.

C: I also have a traveler's cheque of my friend's. He has to stay in hospital for a while at the moment, and so can I cash this cheque on his behalf?

T: I am sorry to hear that. But I am afraid you cannot do it for him. Traveler's cheques can only be accepted from the buyer himself holding his own valid passport, and you can't cash somebody else's traveler's cheque over the counter. I hope that you can understand.

---

inconvenience /ˌɪnkən'viːnjəns/ n. 麻烦,不方便的地方

presence /'prezəns/ n. 出席,到场,存在

Banking English

C: 好吧,也只好这样了。
T: 请您填写兑换水单,并签字。……这是您的护照、钱及水单,请您收好。
C: 谢谢。
T: 别客气。祝您的朋友早日康复。再见!
C: 再见!

NOTES

1. international common practice 国际惯例

   e.g. according to the international common practice 按照国际惯例

2. I am sorry to hear that. 很遗憾得知这个消息。

   当我们听到他人遭遇不幸,或者遇到困难的时候,可以用"I am sorry to hear that." 来表达同情的意思。此外,"遗憾"的类似表达方法还有:What a pity! 真遗憾。(pity n. 令人遗憾的事)

Traveler's Cheques

C: OK, that is fine. Just go on.

T: Please fill in this exchange memo and sign it. ...Here is your passport, your money and the memo.

C: Thanks.

T: You are welcome! And I hope that your friend will be better soon! See you.

C: See you!

中国银行股份有限公司北京经济技术开发区支行
Bank of China Limited Beijing Jingjijishukaifaqu Subbranch

银行英语
Banking English

旅行支票—4

旅支授权及保管水单

在中国银行某支行网点柜台,史密斯先生想要兑付他的旅行支票,由于他希望兑付的旅支总额达到了一定水平,该银行职员需得到旅行支票发行公司的授权后才能兑现。

T: 柜员   C: 客户

T: 您好,请问您办理什么业务?
C: 你好,我可以兑换一些人民币吗?
T: 可以,您换多少?
C: 换2000美元,今天汇率是多少?
T: 100美元兑换人民币799.23元。
C: 我还有5000美元旅行支票想换成人民币。
T: 请您出示您的护照,并在支票上复签。您的复签需要和初签一致。
T: 请您填写水单,另外,我们需要向旅行支票公司要授权,请您稍候。
C: 没问题。(过了一会儿……)
T: 给您,这是兑换的人民币,已经扣除了原币金额0.75%的贴息。
C: 谢谢,如果在我回国时这些人民币没花完,我还可以换回来吗?
T: 可以,两年之内,凭兑换水单,您可以在任何一家中行网点把人民币换回美元的。
C: 噢,我明白了,太感谢你了。
T: 不客气。再见!
C: 再见!

NOTES

1. wait a second 稍等 类似的表达还有:wait a minute, wait a moment 等
2. deduct v. 扣除;减除
   deduct the interest 扣除利息
   e.g. The discount has been deducted already. 您的贴息已经被扣除过了。
   deduction n. 扣除
   相关词组:make a deduction 扣除,扣减

Authorization and Exchange Memo

At a bank counter, Mr. Smith wants to cash his traveler's cheques. As the total amount of his cheques exceeds the regulatory limit, the bank clerk must get the authorization of the T/C issuing company first.

T: Teller   C: Customer

T: Hello, what can I do for you today?
C: Hello, I want to change some money into RMB.
T: Yes, of course. How much would you like to change?
C: Two thousand US dollars. By the way, what is the exchange rate today?
T: It's 799.23 Yuan for 100 US dollars.
C: I also want to cash 5000 US dollars traveler's cheques into RMB.
T: Please show me your passport, and then countersign the cheques here. By the way, your signature should match the original one.
T: Please fill in this exchange memo. Would you please wait a second until we get the authorization from the traveler's cheques service center?
C: No problem. (After a while...)
T: Here is your money; a 0.75% discount of the face value is deducted already.
C: Thank you. If I don't spend all the RMB, can I change them back when I go home?
T: Yes, of course. Within 2 years you can change the unused RMB back into US dollars with your exchange memo.
C: Oh, I know. Thank you very much.
T: My pleasure. Goodbye!
C: Bye!

旅行支票—5

旅支复签及现钞面额

在中国银行的营业柜台，史密斯先生想要兑付他的旅行支票，他还向柜员提出想要些小面额钞票的需求。他们是怎么谈论不同面额的现钞的呢？

　T: 柜员　　C: 客户

T: 你好！请问您办什么业务？

C: 我想兑换一些美国运通公司的旅行支票，给你。

T: 请您复签，然后出示您的护照并填制水单。在复签时请与初签一致。(史密斯先生复签完毕……)对不起，您签错位置了。

C: 好，但是签在哪里？

T: 就在此处印有"当着付款代理人(或出纳人员)的面进行复签"字样的地方。您需要什么面额的现钞？

C: 我需要四张五十元；五张二十元的。其他的可以是百元张的。如果可能的话，您给我，你们国家的硬币各一枚，最好是新的。我留作纪念。

T: 给您。今天的汇率是每100英镑兑1226.70元人民币。您的支票已经兑换成2635.29元人民币，扣除了票面金额0.75%的贴息。这是您需要钱的面额。您很幸运，这是几枚新的硬币，请您保存好。

Countersigning and Asking for Various Banknote Denominations

At a counter of Bank of China, Mr. Smith wants to negotiate his traveler's cheques. He also tells the clerk he wants some small bills. Let us see how they talk about banknotes of various denominations.

T: Teller   C: Customer

T: Good morning! Is there anything I can do for you?

C: I'd like to exchange some American Express traveler's cheques into RMB cash. Here you are.

T: Please countersign them, and then show me your passport and fill out this exchange memo. You know that your signature should be the same as the original one. (After Mr. Smith signed...) Sorry, I'm afraid you signed in the wrong place.

C: Well, but where should I sign?

T: Just here, on the line "countersign here in presence of paying agent (or cashier)". How would you like your money?

C: I need four 50s, five 20s, and the rest in hundreds. If possible, please give me some coins of your country. Just one denomination a piece, and I would very much appreciate if you can give me brand-new ones. I want to keep some as souvenirs of this trip.

T: Wait a second, please. Here you are. By the way, it's RMB1493.38 for GBP 100.00 according to today's rate, so your money comes to RMB 2635.29. A 0.75% of the face value discount has been already deducted. Here are the various denominations of banknotes and coins you required, and these coins are brand-new.

American Express 美国运通
cashier /kəˈʃɪə/ n. 出纳人员
brand-new /brændnjuː/ adj. 全新的，崭新的
souvenir /ˈsuːvənɪə/ n. 纪念品

C: 谢谢您的服务。我一定保存好。
T: 谢谢您！再见！
C: 再见！

NOTES

1. negotiate *v.* 议付（汇票、支票等）

    e.g. negotiating bank 议付行 negotiate a bill 票据交割、让与支票票据议付

    negotiator *n.* 交易人，议付人

    前面单元中,兑现旅行支票常用到的是"cash",相比较"cash"而言,negotiate 比较正式。

2. denomination *n.* （种类、数值或大小的）单位,面值

    e.g. Cash registers have compartments for cash notes of different denominations. 现金注册员把不同面值的钱放在不同的分隔间中。

    e.g. The money comes in ￥20 and ￥50 denominations.

    找您20元和50元两种面值的人民币。

    需要注意的是,denomination 也是比较正式的词语,除非特殊需要,外国客户很少在柜台使用。说到零钱,我们可以用 small bills/notes,或 change 来表达。

    e.g. The discount has been deducted already. 您的贴息已经被扣除过了。

    deduction *n.* 扣除

    相关词组：make a deduction 扣除,扣减

旅行支票
Traveler's Cheques

C: Perfect! I will add them to my collection. Thank you very much for your help.

T: Thank you. Good-bye!

C: Bye-bye!

中国银行股份有限公司北京宣武支行
Bank of China Limited Beijing Xuanwu Subbranch

银行英语
Banking English

旅行支票—6

旅行支票丢失处理

迈克在香港购买的旅行支票不慎丢失了,他来到银行询问旅行支票的相关挂失手续。该银行职员正在帮他办理。

T: 柜员   C: 客户

T: 您好。需要帮忙吗?
C: 是的,我在香港买了些旅行支票,可后来发现丢了。
T: 真为您感到遗憾。看一下您的购买协议好吗?
C: 找不到了。
T: 还记得这些丢失支票的号码吗?
C: 不记得了。
T: 您得找一下购买协议或回忆一下支票号码,然后赶紧和旅行支票公司取得联系。
C: 噢,购买协议找到了,给你。

中国银行股份有限公司北京上地支行
Bank of China Limited Beijing Shangdi Subbranch

Solutions to Lost or Stolen Traveler's Cheques

Mike lost his traveler's cheques he bought in Hong Kong, so he comes to our bank and asks for help. How to report and replace lost or stolen cheques? What should Mike do to get refund?

T: Teller   C: Customer

T: Hello, what can I do for you today?

C: Oh God, I bought some traveler's cheques in Hong Kong, but I can't find them now.

T: I am sorry to hear that, but I think I can help. Would you please give me your purchase agreement?

C: I can't find that either.

T: Then do you remember the serial numbers of the lost traveler's cheques?

C: Sorry, I forgot the serial numbers.

T: I am afraid that you have to get your purchase agreement or the serial numbers of the cheques before you notify the traveler's cheques company of the loss.

C: Uh, I see... maybe I can find it...Oh, I've got the purchase agreement! Here you are.

---

serial number 序列号
lost /lɒst/ *adj.* 丢失的，丧失的；错过的；迷惑的
serial /ˈsɪərɪəl/ *adj.* 连续的

银行英语
Banking English

T: 好的,您的旅行支票是由美国运通发行的,现在您只要与美国运通旅行支票服务中心取得联系,把旅行支票信息、丢失情况以及个人资料告诉服务人员,经他们审核后,会指示您理赔的步骤。按照他们传真过来的授权书和旅行支票遗失索偿的申请表,我们就可以为您办理挂失理赔手续了。

> 迈克拨打了美国运通旅行支票服务中心的客户服务电话,几天之后美国运通公司根据客户所在地理位置,与就近的银行取得了联系,并把授权书、理赔申请表(载有客户的信息资料)传真过去。迈克根据旅行支票公司的提示,前往银行办理理赔。

T: 这份表是旅行支票遗失索偿的申请,请填写一下这份申请表,并在上面签字。
C: 给。
T: 好了,在旅行支票公司的授权下,我们可以给您补偿。
C: 太感谢了!
T: 别客气!

NOTES

1. fill out *v.* 填写(表格等)

    e.g. fill out the application form 填写这份申请表

    fill out 通常是美式英语的表达法,英式英语也常用 fill in 表达同一意思,

    如: fill in the receipt in duplicate 一式两份填这张收据

2. either *adv.* 也(用于否定句,通常置于句末)

    e.g. I don't like the red shirt and I don't like the green one either.

    我不喜欢这件红衬衫,也不喜欢这件绿衬衫。

    "too"是"either"的近义词,但"too"用于肯定句和疑问句中,不用于否定句。

3. assist *v.* 援助,帮助

    assist sb. in doing sth. 协助某人做某事

    e.g. Service center personnel will assist you in determining the best way to obtain a refund.

    服务中心的工作人员会协助您决定获得退款的最佳途径。

4. lost 用于修饰物时是"丢失了的"之意,例如:

    a lost pen 丢失的钢笔 one's lost youth 某人逝去的青春

    需要注意的是,一般不以被动形式表示"某东西被丢失",如表示"我的钱丢了。"通常不说:My money was lost. 正确的说法应是:I lost my money. 同样的意思,我们还可以说:My money is missing(失踪的)。

Traveler's Cheques

T: OK, you see, your traveler's cheques are issued by American Express. Now what you need to do is to contact American Express Traveler's Checks Customer Service Center and tell them all the particulars of the cheques, the loss and your personal information. The company will verify your claims and give you step-by-step instructions for a refund. They will fax an authorization letter and a Refund Claim Form to our bank, and we will assist you in obtaining the refund.

step-by-step /step baɪ step/ adj. 按部就班的
assist /əˈsɪst/ v. 援助, 帮助

Mike telephoned American Express Traveler's checks Customer Service Center. Several days later, the company contacted the nearby bank and faxed the authorization letter and Refund Claim Form with the customer's personal data over to the bank. Mike at the same time was informed by the T/C company to come to the bank for the refund.

T: This is the Refund Claim Form for a refund of your lost American Express traveler's cheque. Please fill out the form and sign your name.
C: Here you are.
T: OK. As we have got the authorization of the issuing company, you can get the refund from our bank.
C: Thanks a million!
T: My pleasure.

Banking English

旅行支票—7

旅行支票不得代签及背书转让

罗伯特先生来到受理旅行支票业务的柜台前,想要代替公司的总经理办理旅行支票的兑付业务。

T: 柜员　　C: 客户

T: 您好!您需要帮忙吗?
C: 我有几张旅行支票需要兑现,你可以为我办理吗?
T: 请您把支票给我看一下。
C: 给你。
T: 噢,运通公司的旅行支票可以接受,看一下您的护照好吗?
T: 您的名字是罗伯特·史密斯,但支票是由查理·凯罗签的,可以告诉我他是谁吗?
C: 他是我的总经理,我是他的秘书。
T: 对不起,您不能代他兑现,因为旅行支票必须由原始购买人复签。
C: 但我是他的秘书,为节省时间,我代他签不行吗?
T: 根据国际惯例,不行。
C: 那我该怎么办?
T: 您可以请您的总经理来这里复签。
C: 他忙得很,恐怕不能来,有其他办法吗?
T: 您最好还是请他抽空亲自来。如果他太忙的话,还有一个别的办法,请他在支票上背书,将支票转让给您。
C: 背书?什么意思?

Countersigning Your Own Traveler's Cheques

Mr. Robert comes to the counter of T/C in Bank of China, and wants to cash some traveler's cheques on behalf of his general manager.

T: Teller   C: Customer

T: Hello! May I help you?
C: I've got several traveler's cheques. Can you cash them for me?
T: Please let me see them.
C: Here you are.
T: Oh, traveler's cheques from American Express are acceptable. May I see your passport?
T: Excuse me, Sir. Your name is Robert Smith, but the cheques were signed by Charlie Karol. May I know who he is?
C: He's my general manager, and I'm his secretary.
T: Sorry, you can't cash them on his behalf, because traveler's cheques must be countersigned by the original buyer.
C: But I'm his secretary. Why can't I countersign for him? You know, we just want to save the time.
T: I am sorry that I can't accept them according to the cashing terms and conditions put forward by American Express, the cheques issuing company.
C: Then what shall I do?
T: You can ask your manager to come and countersign them here himself.
C: But he's very busy. I'm afraid he can't make it. Is there any other way?
T: You'd better ask him to come in person. If he's too busy, another way is that he endorses the cheques to you.
C: Endorse? What does that mean?

secretary /ˈsekrətəri/ n. 秘书

Banking English

T: 他在支票背面写:"付给罗伯特·史密斯先生的指定人,其签字如下:您的签字,然后您总经理的签字:查理·凯罗。"这样就将支票转让给您了。不过,如果旅行支票这样转让给您,恐怕不能立即给您付现,因为我们要向发出行代收,那样需要一个月。

C: 噢,那时间太长了,我回去和他商量一下,谢谢你!

T: 不客气。希望您能够尽快妥善办理这项业务。再见!

C: 再见!

NOTES

1. endorse v. 在(支票)背面签名、背书;赞同,认可

   e.g. endorse the cheque to someone 在支票上背书(在支票背面签字,表示把票据所有权转让给他人),将支票转让给某人

   endorsement n. 背书,在票据上签字(附在保险单上增加条款的便条)

   The congress finally endorsed the national defense budget. 国会最后通过了国防预算。

2. Is there any other way? =Any other means? 有其他办法吗?

旅行支票
Traveler's Cheques

T: "Endorse" means that he writes on the back of the cheque: "Payment made to the designated person of Mr. Robert Smith". The signatures are as follows: your signature, then your manager's signature, "Charlie Karol". Then the cheques are transferred to you. However, if the traveler's cheques are transferred to you like this, there is no immediate cashing, for we need to collect the money from the cheques issuing bank through our corresponding bank, which usually takes a month.

> endorse /ɪnˈdɔːs/ v. 在(支票)背面签名、背书；赞同
> immediate /ɪˈmiːdjət/ adj. 立刻的，直接的，紧接的

C: Oh, that's too long. I'll go back to cheque with him. Thank you anyway.
T: You're welcome. Hope to see you soon. Bye!
C: See you!

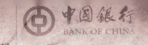

银行英语
Banking English

补充单词

negotiate	/nɪˈgəʊʃɪeɪt/	v.	议付(汇票、支票等)
endorsement	/ɪnˈdɔːsmənt/	n.	背书
apiece	/əˈpiːs/	adv.	每个,每人,各
preferable	/ˈprefərəbəl/	adj.	更可取的,更好的,更优越的
reimburse	/ˌriːmˈbɜːs/	v.	偿还,偿付
prior to			在……之前
acceptable	/əkˈseptəbəl/	adj.	可接受的,受欢迎的

Exercise

I. Fill in the blank

1. According to _____ _____ _____, traveler's cheques can only be accepted with the buyer him or herself holding their own _____ _____.
   根据国际惯例,办理旅行支票必须本人出示其有效的护照。

2. The traveler's cheque must be _____ in _____ of the bank clerk.
   旅行支票必须在银行柜台进行复签。

II. Translation

1. 银行会将你的五美元支票兑付现金。
   _____

2. 我只有这一张100美元的支票。
   _____

3. 在给您兑换支票之前我需要看一下您的护照。
   _____

4. 您不能委托他人做这个业务。
   _____

5. 请先填写申请表。
   _____

6. 您取得您公司的授权了么?
   _____

7. 我们需要扣除您原币金额1%的贴息。
   _____

旅行支票
Traveler's Cheques

8. 现在美元的汇率是 7.8 : 1。
   _____

9. 到那时我可以换回我的钱么？
   _____

10. 我可以看看您的身份证吗？
    _____

11. 我需要些零钱。
    _____

12. 我不要小面额钞票。
    _____

13. 自助取款机把我的卡吞进去了。
    _____

III. Complete the dialogue

G: Foreign Guest　　　　C: Bank Clerk

G: Good morning, Sir. I am George Smith, from America. My Chinese is poor. Can you help me?
   您好，我叫乔治·史密斯，从美国来的。我的中文不好，你可以帮我吗？

C: It's my ____(1)____, what can I do for you?
   当然可以了，我能帮您做点什么？

G: Oh, I need some more cash for my visit in China.
   是这样，我这次来中国钱没带够，想多取点钱。

C: Is it in ____(2)____ ?
   是兑换旅行支票吗？

G: Yes. May I cash a traveler's cheque here?
   是啊！你这能兑换吗？

C: Of course. We'd be happy to cash it for you.
   当然，我很乐意为您兑现。

G: Well, may I ____(3)____ these three cheques of American Express for $100 each? I think that will be enough.
   那么，我能把每张100美元的3张美国运通的支票兑现吗？我想该够用了。

C: Yes, I'll be happy to cash these for you. Would you please ____(4)____ them here?
   好的，我很乐意为你兑换。请您将支票在这里复签一下。

G: Here you are.
   签好了。

C: Could you show me your ____(5)____ ?
   您能把您的护照给我吗？

G: Here it is.

这是我的护照。

C: OK. I will ____(6)____ the exchange memo for you now. Why not take a seat over there for a moment?

好,我现在就为您填写这张兑换水单。您请在那里坐一会儿行吗?

G: I would like to. Thanks.

好的,谢谢。

C: Excuse me, Mr. Smith. I was wondering if you would ever think of ___(7)___ the unused Renminbi back into US dollars later?

您好,史密斯先生,不知道您是否考虑到以后要把没有用完的人民币兑换回美元呢?

G: Yes, if I will have Renminbi left.

是的,如果有没用完的人民币的话,就要换成美元。

C: So, please keep your ___(8)___ and you can return it to the bank when doing the conversion.

那么,我建议您保管好您的这张兑换水单,下次您来办理兑换手续时需要将水单交还给银行。

G: Thank you indeed. I will keep it.

谢谢! 我会保存好水单的。

C: You are welcome. ___(9)___?

不客气。您需要什么面值的货币?

G: Would you please give me twelve one-hundred Yuan notes, ten fifty notes and eight ten notes, and the rest in small change.

请你给我12张100元纸币,10张50元纸币,8张10元纸币,剩下的要零票。

C: Will ten twenty Yuan notes be all right?

10张20元的可以吗?

G: That's all right, but I'd like some coins for a ten Yuan note as ___(10)___.

行,但我想把这张十元纸币换成硬币,留作纪念。

C: ___(11)___. Here is the money you need, and these coins are ___(12)___.

请稍等。这是给您的钱,这些硬币都是全新的,请您拿好。

G: Ok. Thanks a lot.

好的,实在是太感谢了!

C: ___(13)___.

别客气,再见!

第四部分 汇款业务
Part Ⅳ Remittance

汇款业务—1

咨询海外汇款

在中国银行一家网点的大厅里,Waller女士正在向柜员询问有关她国外汇来的款项问题。

T: 柜员　　C: 客户

T: 下午好,女士。能帮您办什么吗?

C: 你好,我叫苏珊·沃勒,我哥哥托尼·沃勒前些天给我汇过来5000英镑,我想查一下它是否到账了。

T: 您有我们银行的存折吗,Waller女士?

C: 有,这是我的存折,我已经让我哥哥直接把钱汇到我的银行账户上了。

T: 我帮您查一下存折余额。非常抱歉,余额显示您的款项还未到账。您还记得您哥哥是什么时候给您汇的款吗?

C: 他上星期三给我打电话的时候告诉我钱已经汇出来了。已经将近一个星期了,你能再帮我查一下吗?

T: 您哥哥告诉您他是用什么方式汇的款吗?

C: 没有,但是他以前汇过很多次,而且一直是用电汇。他给我汇款应该用多长时间?

T: 一般情况下这取决于汇出行,如果汇出行是我们的合作银行,电汇大概需要两天左右,但如果不是,就需要6~7天。您知道您哥哥是从哪家银行给您汇的钱吗?

C: 他一般去巴克莱银行,但我不知道这次是不是。

T: 那您能给我们留下联系电话吗?款项到了以后我们给您打电话。

Checking Inward Remittance

In a branch of Bank of China, Ms. Waller is asking the teller about her remittance from abroad.

T: Teller   C: Customer

T: Good afternoon, Ms. May I help you?

C: Yes, my name is Susan Waller. My brother Tony Waller sent 5,000 pounds to me a few days ago and I want to check if it has arrived.

T: Do you have an account with our bank, Miss Waller?

C: Yes, this is my passbook and I have asked my brother to send the money to my account directly.

T: OK, let me check the balance for you. Well, I'm sorry; it shows that the money hasn't arrived. Do you have any idea when your brother sent you the money?

C: He called me last Wednesday and told me the money had been sent. Now, it's almost a week, could you check it again, please?

T: Did your brother tell you by which method he sent the money?

C: No, he didn't. Previously he used telegraphic transfer. How long does it take if he sends the money by telegraphic transfer?

T: It depends, normally, if the remitting bank is one of our correspondent banks, it will take about 2 working days. But if the remitting bank is not our correspondent bank, it will take 6 to 7 working days. Do you know from which bank your brother sent the money to you?

C: Normally, he goes to Barclays Bank, but I am not sure about it this time.

T: Could you tell us your telephone number? We will call you as soon as the money arrives.

account /əˈkaʊnt/ n. 账户
check /tʃek/ v. 检查,查证,核实
balance /ˈbæləns/ n. 余额
remit /rɪˈmɪt/ v. 汇出

Banking English

C: 你们真是太好了。我的电话是 64931259,我急需这笔钱,如果有了什么消息请立即给我打电话。谢谢你们。

T: 不客气。我们会及时和您联系的。

一天之后,柜员打电话联系沃勒女士……

T: 您好!请找苏珊·沃勒女士。

C: 我就是。

T: 您好,沃勒女士,您的汇款已经到账,您可以到银行来办理手续了。

C: 我马上过去,太感谢你们了。

NOTES

1. remit vt. 汇款,汇寄

   e.g. Please remit payment by cheque immediately. 请以支票汇出。
   remittance 汇出的款

   e.g. The mother sends her daughter a small remittance each month.
   母亲每月给她的女儿汇一小笔钱。

2. telegraphic transfer (TT) 银行电汇   demand draft (DD) 票汇
   mail transfer (MT) 信汇

3. normally 通常情况下

   e.g. Normally we cannot process the transaction, but we can apply for exception.
   通常我们不能办理这笔业务,但可以申请例外处理。

4. It depends on... 视……而定

   e.g. The speed of the remittance also depends on the bank's system.
   汇款的速度还取决于银行内部系统。

Remittance

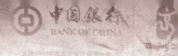

C: That is very kind of you. My phone number is 64931259. Please call me if there is any news about the money, you know, I really need it. Thank you for your help.

T: You are welcome. We will contact you as soon as the money arrives.

One day later, the teller calls Ms. Waller...

T: Hello, this is Bank of China. May I speak to Ms. Susan Waller, please?

C: Yes, speaking.

T: Hello, Ms. Waller, your money has just arrived. Now you can come to our branch to withdraw it.

C: OK! I will come right away. Thank you very much.

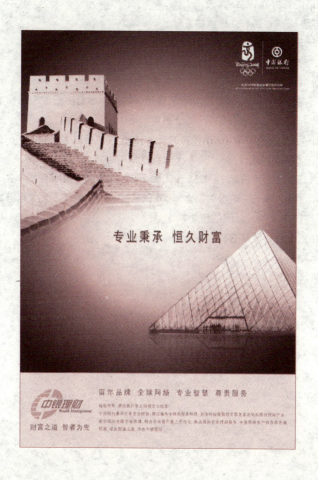

汇款业务—2

汇款手续费与定期自动转存

沃勒女士收到了一笔国外汇款,她打算怎样处理这笔钱呢?

T: 柜员　　**C**: 客户

T: 您好,请问您办理什么业务?
C: 我是苏珊·沃勒,我来办理我的汇款。
T: 您好,沃勒女士,您的汇款已到账,有 20 英镑的国际清算费用,实际入账是 4980 英镑,您想怎么办理?
C: 这个费用太高了。
T: 20 英镑是银行对国际清算所收取的费用。这是对所有客户收取的标准费用。如果汇出行是我们的合作银行,这个费用则是 10 英镑。
C: 噢,明白了。那我就取 1000 英镑的现金,500 英镑换成人民币,剩下的钱存成英镑的定期存款。顺便问一下,今天的英镑汇率是多少?
T: 今天的汇率是 1 英镑换 14.9255 元人民币。这样您的 500 英镑可以换 7462.75 元人民币。请您填一下这份兑换水单,并让我看一下您的护照。请问您想把剩下的 3480 英镑存成多长时间的定期?
C: 我想存一个月自动转存的定期。

Remittance Commission and Making a Time Deposit

Ms. Waller has received her money from abroad in Bank of China Beijing branch. Now what does she plan to do with the money?

T: Teller   C: Customer

T: Good morning, Miss, what can I do for you?

C: Good morning, I am Susan Waller and I want to know whether my money's arrived?

T: OK, let me see. Yes, your money has arrived. But there will be a 20-pound bank charge for international clearing, so you will only receive 4,980 pounds. How would you like to have it?

C: This is too expensive.

T: Well, the 20 pounds are the bank charges for international clearing. This is the standard charge for all customers. But if the remitting bank is one of our correspondent banks, the handling fee will be just 10 pounds.

C: Oh, I see. Well, I want to have 1,000 pounds in cash, 500 pounds in RMB and as for the rest, please make it a time deposit for me. By the way, what is the exchange rate today for pounds?

T: That is 100 pounds for 1,492.55 RMB. So you can get 7,462.75 RMB for the 500 pounds. Please fill in this exchange memo, and let me have a look at your passport. And what about the rest of the money, say, 3,480 pounds. How long would you like to deposit it?

C: Well, I'd like a one-month deposit, automatically renewed if I don't give the bank further instruction.

charge /tʃɑːdʒ/ n. 费用
   v. 要价(要定量的钱)作为收费
correspondent /ˌkɒnˈspɒndənt/ adj.
   相关的,相应的
exchange /ɪksˈtʃeɪndʒ/ v. 交换,交易,
   兑换
memo /ˈmeməʊ/ n. 备忘录

银行英语
Banking English

T: 好的。这是您的存单、兑换水单、7000元人民币和1000英镑,请您清点一下。我再给您一个我行全球合作银行的清单,这样您哥哥下次汇款时就可以考虑去其中的任何一家银行办理了。

C: 我要告诉我哥哥下次去你们的合作银行办理。那一定很有用。谢谢你。

T: 不用谢,再见。

C: 再见!

NOTES

1. 有关国际汇款在柜台服务时经常用到的主要各方:

   remitting bank 汇款行

   correspondent bank 往来行

   intermediary bank 中转行

   beneficiary/beneficiary's bank 收款行/汇入行

   receiving/paying bank 解付行

   clearing bank 清算行

   remitter 汇款人

   receiver/recipient/beneficiary 收款人

1. 手续费:haudling fee; processing fee.

Remittance

T: OK. Now here is your time deposit certificate, exchange memo and your cash in RMB and 1,000 pounds sterling. Please check them. Let me give you a list of our correspondent banks all over the world, and your brother may consider using any one of them for future remittance.

C: I will let my brother use your correspondent bank next time. That is very useful. Thank you.

T: You are welcome. Good-bye.

C: Good-bye.

exchange memo 兑换水单
correspondent bank 代理行
remittance /rɪˈmɪtəns/ n. 汇款

中国银行股份有限公司北京丰台支行
Bank of China Limited Beijing Fengtai Subbranch

Banking English

汇款业务—3

汇入查询二例

一位女士正在中国银行北京市分行查询国外的汇入汇款。同时,对一些问题她存在很多疑虑,所以正在问询更多的信息。

T: 柜员   C: 客户

例1　查询余额

T: 请问您办理什么业务?
C: 我有一笔汇款,请帮我看一下到了吗?
T: 请问您知道汇出时间和金额吗?
C: 时间是2006年9月15日,大概是2000美元。
T: 对不起,汇款没到,汇款一般3至5个工作日到账。
C: 谢谢!再见!
T: 再见!

例2　中转银行手续费

T: 您有什么需要帮忙的么?
C: 您好!我有一笔汇款已经到了,少了50美元,帮我查一下吧。
T: 请您不必担心,这是中转行扣除的费用。
C: 为什么?

Two Examples of Checking Inward Remittance

A lady is checking her inward remittance in Bank of China Beijing branch. Meanwhile, there is something she cannot quite understand, so she is asking for further information.

T: Teller   C: Customer

Example One   Checking Balance

T: Good afternoon, what can I do for you?
C: I've had some money wired here from abroad several days ago. Would you please check it for me?
T: When was the money wired and how much?
C: It was on Sep. 15th, 2006 and the amount was about 2,000 U.S. dollars.
T: Sorry, the money has not arrived yet. Generally speaking, it takes about 3—5 working days to reach Bank of China.
C: Thank you. Good-bye.
T: Good-bye.

Example Two   Intermediary Bank Commission

T: Good morning, what can I do for you?
C: Good morning, I have received some money from abroad, but I think there is 50 dollars less.
T: Please do not worry about it. That is the charge from the intermediary bank.

> intermediary /ˌɪntəˈmiːdɪərɪ/ *adj.* 中间的, 媒介的

银行英语
Banking English

T: 是这样的,您的汇款行和中行没有直接账户关系,要由汇款行找一家与中行有账户关系的银行。这家银行就是中间行,也就是中转行。我给您看一下国外的电报吧。

C: 原来是这样的。看来下次汇款要找一家和中行有关系的银行。

T: 我们中国银行在海外有许多分支机构,欢迎到中国银行办理业务。

C: 一定的。谢谢!再见!

T: 再见!

NOTES

1. as soon as: conj. 一……就
   e.g. I'll write you back as soon as I get there.
   我一到那儿,就给你回信。

2. ring up: 打电话
   e.g. Last evening I was rung up by an old friend whom I had not heard of for years.
   昨晚一位老朋友打电话给我,我多年没听到他的消息了。

3. direct banking relationship 直接代理行关系

4. commission 手续费 也作 handling charge, service charge

5. good choice 很好的选择
   e.g. Bank of China will be your best choice.
   中国银行将是您的最佳选择。

Remittance

C: Could you please tell me why?

T: OK. Because there is no direct banking relationship between the remitting bank and Bank of China, the remitting bank will have to choose an intermediary bank, which has the relationship with our bank, to transfer the money to our bank. So, that 50 dollars is the charge by the intermediary bank. I will show you the telegraph of the money transfer.

C: OK, I see. Next time, I will tell my friend to go to one of your correspondent banks.

T: Bank of China has a global network. So our overseas branch would be a good choice to make the money transfer.

C: Of course. Thank you, Good-bye.

T: Good-bye.

中国银行股份有限公司北京密云支行
Bank of China Limited Beijing Miyun Subbranch

银行英语
Banking English

汇款业务—4

解释汇款名称不符的问题

绝大多数情况下,收款行会完全依照付款指令或电汇报文上所显示的收款人姓名和账号入账,一旦报文上的姓名或是账号与收款人在收款行开立的账户相关信息不符,银行会暂缓入账。现在,一位柜员正向客户说明这方面的规定。

T: 柜员　　C: 客户

T: 您好,我能为您做些什么?
C: 9月12日我朋友从美国汇了5000美元给我,已经15天了,为什么还没有到账?
T: 请您稍等,我帮您查询一下。(片刻)对不起,让您久等了,您这笔款项由于姓名不符不能入账,您看汇款单上的收款人姓名为MARKAR,而您的账户户名为MARKER,我看看您的护照,也是MARKER,我们已经向汇款行进行查询,待查复更正后就可入账。
C: 为什么?这钱确实是我的呀!

中国银行股份有限公司北京奥运村支行
Bank of China Limited Beijing Aoyuncun Subbranch

Dealing with Non-Compliance of Account Name and Number

In most cases, the beneficiary bank is entitled to credit the money wired from abroad to the client's account based only on the client's account number indicated in the payment order or wire telegraph. Any non-compliance of the account number and name of the recipient indicated in the payment order would lead to a suspension of money transfer. Now a teller is trying to explain to a customer about the regulations in this regard.

T: Teller   C: Customer

T: Good afternoon. Can I help you?

C: My friend wired me 5,000 dollars from America on September 12th. Now 15 days have passed, why haven't I got it?

T: Would you wait a moment, please? I will check it for you. (A few minutes later) Sorry to keep you waiting. Here is the problem. Your remittance cannot be credited, as the names are not identical. You see, the recipient's name on the remittance form is "MARKAR", while your account name here in our bank is "MARKER". And can I take a look at your passport?

... See? It is also "M-A-R-K-E-R". I guess that is the problem on the remittance. We have faxed an inquiry letter to the remitting bank, and if we got the confirmation from them, your remittance will be credited immediately.

C: Why bother? The money is mine, just give it to me.

> beneficiary /ˌbenɪ'fɪʃəri/ n. 收款人，受益人
> identical /aɪ'dentɪkəl/ adj. 相同的，同一的

银行英语
Banking English

T: 非常抱歉!银行有规定:接受汇款必须户名、账号完全一致才能入账,这是银行为保证客户资金安全而采取的一项措施,希望您能理解。

C: 如果我朋友发一份传真给银行进行更正,行吗?

T: 对不起,不可以。银行只接受汇款银行通过银行内部渠道传送的更正信息。我们也会催汇出行尽快给我行回复查询结果,一旦收到查询答复,我们会马上通知您。

C: 那现在我能做些什么呢?

T: 您也可以联系汇款人让他到汇款行主动进行更正,将收款人姓名更正为MARKER,这样时间可能会快一些。

C: 好吧,照你说的做。谢谢!

T: 不客气。

C: 再见!

T: 再见!

NOTES

1. keep sb. waiting 让某人等候
2. 关于国际汇款,我们最先想到的也许是 remit 或是 remittance,不少人最初是通过电子词典或有关国际结算业务的金融英语书籍接触到这个词。remit 当然是"汇款"较为贴切的翻译,但在柜台交流时,我们却很少听到外国客人这么说,他们可能会说 wire, send,还有 transfer,但就是很少说 remit。为什么呢?多数字典除了告诉我们 remit 的中文含意外,还会告诉我们,remit 是个"较正式(formal)"的词。换句话说,书面语可能会经常使用,而口语却不那么经常使用了。总之,编者举 remit 这个例子是想说明,我们学习英语不仅要记住某个单词的具体含义,还要揣摩每个词的使用场合,在实际交流过程中,用简单的英语讲复杂的事情是我们的目标。

Remittance

T: Terribly sorry. According to the regulations of our bank, the remittance can be credited only on the basis of full compliance of the account name and the account number. This is a practice to guarantee the safety of our customers' money and to prevent operational risk. I hope you could understand.

> urge /ɜːdʒ/ v. 驱策,力劝,力陈
> inform /ɪnˈfɔːm/ vt. 通知,告诉,向……报告
> response /rɪˈspɒns/ n. 反应,回答,响应
> situation /ˌsɪtjuˈeɪʃən/ n. 情况

C: What about my friend sending a fax to your bank to correct it? Would that be OK?

T: Sorry, I am afraid not. The bank only accepts the revised version from the remitting bank through our special internal channel. We will urge your friend's bank to reply to our inquiry, and we will inform you as soon as we get the response.

C: Well, what should I do now?

T: You can contact your friend, and ask him to go to his bank, explain about the situation and make it "M-A-R-K-E-R" directly. That, perhaps, would make it faster.

C: All right, I will do that. Thank you.

T: You are welcome!

C: Good-bye!

T: Bye-bye!

汇款业务—5

合格汇票的兑付与托收

银行汇票是一种由银行签发的,委托付款人在见票时无条件支付确定的金额给收款人或者持票人的一种金融工具。现在,一个外国人持一张海外银行开出的汇票前来我行兑现,银行职员解释了我行直接付款和承兑托收汇票的差别,并介绍了兑付汇票的基本手续。

T: 柜员　C: 客户

例 1　兑付

T: 早安。能为您做些什么?
C: 我这儿有一张1000美元的汇票,我想把它取出来。
T: 给我看一下汇票好吗?
C: 在这儿。是从美国一家公司寄来的。
T: 噢,是纽约汇丰银行开出的。
C: 是的,这是一家信誉很好的银行。
T: 是以我行为付款人的,现在可以兑现,但须先根据我们的签字样本核对一下印鉴。
C: 好的。有什么费用吗?

Remittance

Cashing and Collection of a Bank Draft

Unit 5

A bank draft is a financial instrument which is issued by a bank, allowing the individual named on the draft to receive a specified amount of cash on demand. Now a foreigner takes a bank draft issued by a foreign bank to Bank of China and asks to cash it. A bank clerk first explains to him the difference between the draft drawn on our bank and the draft for collection. And then he introduces the basic procedures to cash a bank draft.

T: Teller   C: Customer

Example One   Cashing

T: Good morning, what can I do for you?

C: I've got a 1,000 U.S. dollar cheque here. I would like to cash it.

T: Could you show me your check?

C: Here it is. It is from an American company.

T: I see. This is a bank draft drawn by the HSBC New York.

C: Yes, it is a bank with a good **reputation**.

T: Well, the draft is drawn on us and we can cash it for you right now. But what we need to do first is to **verify** the **signature** on the draft against our **specimen**, is that all right?

C: OK. Are there any charges for cashing it?

T: No.

C: But I remember last time you charged me some money for cashing a cheque like that.

---

reputation /ˌrepjuˈteɪʃən/ n. 名誉,名声
verify /ˈverɪfaɪ/ v. 证明,确定
signature /ˈsɪɡnətʃə/ n. 签名
specimen /ˈspesɪmɪn/ n. 样本,标本

Banking English

T: 没有。
C: 但上次你们扣减了一些费用。
T: 托收的汇票是要收取费用的。如果汇票是以我行为付款行的,就可以直接办理兑付手续,如果是以其他银行为付款行的,我们只能寄给付款银行办理托收,并且我们要收取一定量的手续费。不过现在您的汇票明确指定我行为付款行,所以我们可以为您直接兑付,并且不收手续费。
C: 托收费用怎么收?
T: 是汇票金额的 1‰,按卖出价折成人民币。
T: 现在请您填写这份水单好吗?
C: 当然。(找他的眼镜),但今天我忘记带眼镜啦。请替我填好吗?
T: 好的。不过请在这儿填好你的姓名,在这儿填好金额,我来替你填写汇率及人民币金额。
C: 谢谢!
T: 先生,您的钱在这儿。请您收好,再见!
C: 再见!

例2 托收

T: 早安,能帮您忙吗?
C: 我这儿有一张 2000 美元的支票。能给我兑付吗?
T: 噢,是一张个人支票,付款人是纽约渣打银行。
C: 是的。也许您可以立刻给我付现。
T: 很抱歉,不能立即付现,但我们可以给您办理托收。收妥时我们会及时通知您。
C: 为什么?
T: 我们不能肯定出票人是否有足够的余额。

Remittance

T: Maybe you are talking about a cheque collection. Normally, if the check is not drawn on us, or in other words, if our bank is not the designated paying bank on the cheque, we have to first send it back by post to the duly paying bank for money collection before you can actually get paid. In this case certain bank fee is charged. But now your check does specify that our bank is the drawee or, the paying bank, so it is payable on demand and we can cash it for you without any charge.

> drawee /drɔː'iː/ n. (支票、汇票等的)付款人
> convert /kən'vɜːt/ v. 兑换，折换
> exchange rate 汇率
> payer /'peɪə/ n. 付款人
> collection /kə'lekʃən/ n. 托收

C: How much do you charge for the collection?

T: It is 0.1% of the draft amount, converted into RMB at the selling rate.

T: Now, could you fill out this memo, please?

C: Sure, (looking for his glasses) sorry, I forgot to bring my glasses, could you fill it out for me?

T: Certainly, Sir. But please sign your name here and the check amount here and I will write the exchange rate and the RMB amount for you.

C: Thanks a lot.

T: Here is your money, Sir. Have a good day! Good-bye!

C: Good-bye!

Example Two   Collection

T: Good morning, can I help you?

C: I'd like to cash a cheque for two thousand U.S. dollars.

T: Oh, it's a personal cheque. The payer is Standard Chartered, New York Branch.

C: Yes, it is. Now would you cash it for me?

T: I'm sorry, we cannot cash it for you immediately, but we can collect it for you. And we can give you a call as soon as the money arrives.

C: Why is that?

T: Because we're not sure whether the cheque issuer has enough balance with the bank or not.

Banking English

C: 出票人是我的一个好朋友。他说话一直是算数的。

T: 我不怀疑这一点，但我们要得到证实后才能付款。最好的解决办法是我们现在就办理托收手续。

C: 不能照顾一下吗？我就要离开上海了。

T: 您还回来吗？

C: 大约一个月以后。

T: 如果一切都顺利的话，相信可以在一个月后收妥。

C: 好吧！就按你说的办。

T: 托收的钱回来后，我们会打电话通知您。

C: 谢谢，再见！

T: 再见！

NOTES

1. drawn by 由……开出的
   drawn on 由……承兑的
2. in other words 换句话说
3. 本小节中提到了一些和票据清算有关的当事人和表达一般票据行为的单词，下面就是一些最基本的相关词汇。

   drawer 出票人   drawee 付款人   payee 收款人
   issue 出票   address 签发   endorsement 背书
   presentation 提示 acceptance 承兑 payment 付款
   dishonor 拒付   bounce 退票   recourse 追索
   verity 证实   certify 出具证明

4. cash 作动词表示"兑现，抵用"，这一意义上的名词形式为 cashing 或 encashment。

Remittance

C: The issuer is my good friend. He is a creditworthy person.

T: I believe you. But we'll not credit your account until the balance is verified. And the best way is that we start the check collection procedures now.

C: Would you please do me a favor? I'm going to leave Shanghai very soon.

T: Will you be back?

C: I'll be back in one month.

T: If everything is all set, you can receive your money in one month.

C: OK, please do as you've suggested.

T: We will inform you by phone when the money arrives.

C: Thanks. Bye-bye!

T: Bye!

procedure /prə'siːdʒə/ n. 手续

中国银行股份有限公司北京昌平支行
Bank of China Limited Beijing Changping Subbranch

银行英语
Banking English

汇款业务—6

非居民客户向海外汇款

一位女士通过电话向中国银行的一名大堂经理询问有关向国外汇款的问题。

M: 大堂经理   C: 客户

M: 您好,您需要什么帮助吗?
C: 你好,女士。我想往加拿大汇一笔钱。我有你们银行的外币账户。我应该怎么办理?
M: 请问您准备汇多少钱?账户是钞户还是汇户?
C: 我想汇 85000 加元到温哥华。是汇户。钞户、汇户有什么区别吗?
M: 外币现汇户是指由境外汇入的款项,而外币现钞户是指存取外币现金的账户。对于国际汇款,不同性质的账户费用不同。例如,如果您从现汇户取款,您需要支付两种费用:电报费和手续费;而您若从现钞户汇款,您还需另外支付差价费。
C: 原来是这样。
M: 您是想用电汇还是票汇将钱汇出?
C: 不是特别着急,我想用票汇,这样会便宜一些,对吗?
M: 对,如果您用这种方式汇款将省去 150 元的电报费。
C: 我可以到你们网点用美元换加元吗?

Outward Remittance by Non-Residents

A lady is calling Bank of China to ask about outward remittance.

M: Manager C: Customer

M: Hello! Bank of China. What can I do for you?

C: I want to send some money to Canada. I have a foreign currency account in your bank. What should I do?

M: May I know how much money you would like to send and which kind of account you have in our bank, foreign exchange account or cash account?

C: I want to send 85,000 Canadian dollars to Vancouver and my account is an exchange account. By the way, what is the difference between an exchange account and a cash account?

M: A foreign exchange account is an account to receive money sent from abroad and a foreign cash account is one to deposit and withdraw cash in foreign currencies. When you send money from different types of accounts, the bank charges are different. For example, if you want to transfer some money from your foreign exchange account, there're two kinds of fees: cable charge and processing charge. Whereas, if you use a foreign cash account, there is an extra charge for remitting cash abroad.

C: Oh, I see.

M: How would you like to send the money, by telegraphic transfer or by demand draft?

C: It is no hurry; I'd like to use the draft. It is cheaper, isn't it?

M: Yes, it is. If you use demand draft, you will save 150 RMB of cable charges.

C: Can I go to your branch to change U.S. dollars into Canadian dollars?

Banking English

M：您可以在周一至周五来我们网点办理,也可以到您就近的网点办理。
C：我明白了,我可能在午餐前就会过去,谢谢你的帮助。
M：欢迎您到我们这里办理。再见!
C：再见!

NOTES

1. foreign exchange/remittance account 现汇户
   foreign banknotes/cash account 现钞户
2. What is the difference between ... and... 某物与某物之间的区别是什么
3. There is no hurry. 不急。
4. demand draft 银行汇票,简称 DD
5. any of our branches 我行的任何网点
   some of our branches 我行的某些网点

Remittance

M: Yes, you can do this transaction from Monday to Friday at our branch or at any one of the branches near your home.

C: OK, I see. Maybe I will go before lunch time. Thank you for your help.

M: You're welcome and I'm looking forward to seeing you at our branch. Good-bye!

C: Good-bye!。

中国银行股份有限公司北京延庆支行
Bank of China Limited Beijing Yanqing Subbranch

银行英语
Banking English

汇款业务——7

汇出汇款业务操作与填单辅导

　　汇款通常有三种方式,电汇、信汇和票汇,其中电汇和票汇在国际汇款中最为常用。这两种办法各有优缺点。所以,当一位客户希望向国外汇款的时候,我们首先就要问清他真正的需求是什么。他希望汇款能够快速到账还是更愿意以低廉的价格进行汇款?之后,另一个可能遇到的问题就是,这位客户能够提供哪些有用信息呢?他是否知道环球同业银行金融电讯协会编码、国际银行账号或是检索编码都是什么?如果汇款人只知道收款人的姓名,可能更为适合他汇款的方式就是票汇了。下面我们就来看看银行柜员是如何向客户解释相关规定和银行的操作惯例的。

 T: 柜员　　C: 客户

T: 早上好,先生,请问您要办理什么业务?
C: 早上好,我想向国外汇款。
T: 好的,那么,您是想做电汇还是票汇?
C: 有什么不同吗?
T: 对于收款人而言,电汇是最便捷的收款方式。如果您要选择票汇方式,您还要邮寄或自带汇票给收款人。

Remittance Operation and Guiding Customers with Application

The instruments of remittance include telegraphic transfer(TT), mail transfer(MT), and demand draft (DD), among which telegraphic transfer and demand draft are used most commonly. Both methods have advantages and disadvantages. So when a customer intends to make an international money transfer, it is the priority for us to figure out what he cares about most. Does he want to save time or does he want to save money? And then, another question perhaps would pop up, what kind of information can this customer provide? Does he have all the necessary information to make a telegraphic transfer? Does he have any idea about the swift code, IBAN, or sort code? If he only knows the name of the beneficiary, perhaps a demand draft would be a better option than a telegraphic transfer. Now let us see how a teller explains all these regulations and banking practices to a customer.

T: Teller   C: Customer

T: Good morning! Sir, what can I do for you?
C: Good morning! I want to transfer some money abroad.
T: OK, then which kind of methods do you prefer? Telegraphic transfer or demand draft?
C: What's the difference between them?
T: For the receiver, telegraphic transfer is one of the most convenient and efficient methods to get payment. If you choose the draft, however, you need to mail it to the receiver or take it to him by yourself, which obviously takes a longer time than telegraphic transfer.

payment /ˈpeɪmənt/ n. 付款, 支付, 报酬

Banking English

C: 好吧,那就电汇吧。11000美元,怎么样。

T: 好的,先生,请问您是外币现金汇款还是外币现汇汇款?

C: 我付外币现金。

T: 好的,先生。按照我国外汇管理局规定,超过10,000美元的需要提供一下本人入境申报单,护照或本人原有款银行的外币现钞提取单据。

C: 我今天忘记带入境申报单了,那我汇5000美元吧。哦,这是我的护照。

T: 好的,另外,先生,请您填写一下海外电汇申请书以及对外付款申报单。

C: 好的,不过您能帮我指导一下吗?

T: 当然。这里,先生,请您填写付款人姓名、付款金额、收款人开户银行名称、地址、银行编码,以及收款人姓名。

C: 好的。

T: 这里,先生,结算方式、付款币种、金额,还有国际收支交易编码、交易附言。

C: 好的。

T: 最后,这里,请您签上您的名字好吗?

C: 好的。

T: 先生,都办妥了。

C: 是吗,太感谢了。

T: 别客气,欢迎您再次光临。

C: 谢谢。再见!

NOTES

1. BOP,意为 balance of payment 国际收支。

2. 本小节中提到的 bank code 银行代码,其实只是个较为笼统的说法,具体说来,我们经常会用到的 bank code 包括:

    SWIFT CODE: Society for Worldwide Interbank Financial Telecommunication Code 环球同业银行金融电讯协会编码

    IBAN Number: International Bank Account Number 国际银行账号

    BIC: Bank Identification Code 银行识别码

    ABA Number: American Banker Association Number 美国银行家协会编码

    Sort Code: 英国境内银行代号

    Bank State Branch (BSB): 澳洲境内银行代号

    Transit Number: 加拿大境内银行代号

3. receiving bank 受款行 receiving party 受款方,一般称 beneficiary L/C项下即为受益人 insurance policy 保险单项下即为获得保险赔付的一方

Remittance

C: OK. Let's wire the money then. Say, 11,000 dollars?

T: OK, Sir. Would you like to pay by cash or would you like to use the money in your foreign exchange account?

C: I'd like to pay cash.

T: OK, Sir, according to the foreign exchange control regulations of our country, the maximum amount that you are allowed to transfer is 10,000 dollars per day, and if you want to transfer more than 10,000 dollars, you need to present your passport and also the foreign currency declaration form that you made when you passed the customs or the receipt you got when you withdrew foreign currency in China.

C: I forgot to bring it with me. Well, then I'll just transfer 5,000 dollars. Here is my passport.

T: OK, in addition, Sir, please fill out this application form for Overseas Telegraphic Transfer and this declaration document for foreign payments.

C: OK, can you tell me how to fill it out?

T: Fine. For this application form, please write your name and the amount here in this box, and then the receiving bank's name, address plus the bank code here in this box, and finally, the receiver's name here.

C: No problem.

T: Here, Sir, for this declaration document, you should write things like the payment method, currency of payment, amount of payment, BOP transaction code and transaction remarks.

C: OK.

T: Finally, please sign your name here.

C: Fine, here we go...

T: Sir, everything is done.

C: Really? Thanks a lot.

T: It's my pleasure. Welcome to our bank again.

C: Thanks. Bye-bye!

第五部分 信用卡业务
Part V Credit Card

银行英语
Banking English

信用卡业务—1

申请中银长城国际卡

一位外国客户来到中国银行某网点询问申请信用卡的相关程序。在下面的对话当中,一位银行职员会为他详细地解释办理信用卡所需提供的证明材料和有关预存保证金的相关事宜。

T: 柜员　　C: 客户

T: 您好,请问您需要帮助吗?
C: 您好,我想申请一张中国银行的信用卡,可以进行国际及网上支付的。
T: 没问题。中国银行现在有长城国际卡符合您的需求。
C: 那需要什么手续呢?
T: 您需要填写国际卡申请表格,并提供以下证明文件:(一)本人有效护照复印件;(二)《外国人居留证》复印件;您的《外国人居留证》有效期应在1年(含)以上,且距到期日应在1个月以上;(三)您本人名下在京房产证明;(四)收入证明。如您无法满足上述任意条件,则需要交纳一定数额的保证金。
C: 什么是保证金?
T: 保证金是一种您在银行的财力证明。银行会根据您交的保证金数额给您相应的透支额度。同时您缴存的保证金银行会给您按一年的定期存款记息,到期连本带息自动转存。
C: 那我什么时候可以取回这笔钱?
T: 直到您取消这张信用卡为止。
C: 我明白了。那我需要2000美元的透支额度需多少保证金?保证金是用人民币还是外币交呢?
T: 人民币,美元都可以。如果您用人民币,那么保证金和您的透支额度的比例为10:1,即您交纳20000元人民币可以获得2000美元的透支额。如果您用美元交纳,则为1:1,即您交纳2000美元的保证金就可获得2000美元的额度。
C: 我懂了,那我交完保证金后,多久可以拿到卡?
T: 大概需要10至15个工作日。

Applying for a BOC Great Wall International Card

A foreigner comes to a sub branch of Bank of China and asks about the bank's international credit card application procedures. In the following conversation, one bank clerk will make a full explanation of the documents the foreign customer should present and the initial deposit he has to make.

T: Teller   C: Customer

T: Good morning, Sir. What can I do for you?

C: Hello, I'd like to apply for a credit card in your bank for internet payment.

T: No problem. Well, our Great Wall international credit card is a good choice for you.

C: Good. How can I apply for it?

T: You need to fill out an application form and make an initial deposit as well as provide the following documents. First, we need a copy of your passport. Second, we need a copy of your Foreign Residence Certificate. The term of your residence certificate should be no less than one year and the time from the current date to the expiration date sould be more than 1 month. Third, we need a copy of your local reference's ID card.

C: Would you please tell me what that initial deposit is?

T: Sure. The bank will decide your credit limit according to the amount of initial deposit you make. The interest on the deposit is the same as that of our one-year term deposit and the principal plus the accrued interest will be automatically renewed on the maturity date.

C: But when can I take out my money?

Banking English

C: 好的,等我拿来保证金我会尽快来办卡的,谢谢!
T: 别客气。希望再次见到您。
C: 再见!
T: 再见!

NOTES

1. Would you please...? "你可以……吗?" 一个用来向他人表示请求的句型,语气较为礼貌友好,需要注意的是 please 后面使用的动词都是动词原型。例句如下:

   e.g. Would you please tell me what that deposit is? 请问什么是保证金?

   e.g. Would you please open the door for me? 你可以帮我开一下门吗?

   此外,"Would you mind...?" "你介意……吗?" 也是用来表示请求,希望征得他人同意时经常用到的句型。值得注意的是,mind 后面的动词需要使用 -ing 形式。例如:

   e.g. Would you mind waiting outside for a moment?
   麻烦你在外面等一会儿好吗?

2. credit limit/line 授信额度,这个词组经常用来描述信用卡的透支额度。

3. ratio 的用法:ratio 意为"比,比率,比值"。与之经常搭配在一起使用表示此事务与彼事务之比的是介词 to。例如:

   e.g. The ratio of boys to girls is 3:1. 男孩儿与女孩儿的比例是 3 比 1。(3:1 读作 three to one)

   e.g. The chart shows the ratio of personal debt to personal income. 图表显示的是个人收支比。

4. 关于外籍人办卡所需材料,在提交保证金的前提下,申请人还需要提供的材料包括:

   (1) 本人有效护照 passport

   (2) 外国人居留证 Residence Certificate for Foreigners

   此外,外国人居留许可 Foreigner Residence Permit, 外国人永久居留证 Permanent Residence Certificate for Foreigners 从效力上类似于外国人居留证,也是在办理信用卡时可以提交的有效证明。

   (3) 本地联系人身份证复印件 a copy of a local reference's ID card

5. principal 本金 interest 利息

   The principal bears interest. 本金产生利息。

Credit Card

T: You can get it back when you cancel the card.

C: I see. Well, if I want a 2,000 US dollars credit line, how much shall I deposit first? Shall I pay RMB or dollars?

T: Both are OK. If you pay RMB, the ratio of the amount of deposit to the credit limit is 10:1. That is to say, you need to deposit 20,000 RMB to get a 2,000 US dollars credit limit; and if you pay US dollars, the ratio is 1:1, that is...um... 2,000 US dollars initial deposit for a 2000 US dollars credit line.

C: OK. How long will it take to get the credit card after I make the deposit?

T: It takes about 10—15 working days.

C: All right then. I'll come back to apply for the card some other day because I don't have enough money at the moment. Thanks anyway!

T: You are welcome, hope to see you again.

C: Good-bye!

T: Good-bye!

银行英语
Banking English

信用卡业务—2

办理中银信用卡

中银信用卡是依照国际标准设计的可在全球范围内使用的双币信用卡。一位住在北京的外国客人也打算拥有一张这样的信用卡。办卡时需要向银行提供什么证明材料？多长时间才能拿到新卡？免息期有多长？关于办卡他有很多问题，现在，一位在银行卡服务中心的职员正在为他一一解答。

T: 柜员　　C: 客户

T: 这是中国银行顾客服务中心，我是凯瑟琳，请讲。
C: 我是住在北京的加拿大人，想在贵行办一张信用卡，可以吗？如何申请？
T: 如您能满足以下条件，就可以申请。在京有一份稳定的收入且工作业绩良好，并可提供本人名下在京的房产证明。
C: 以上条件我都满足，那我如何申请？
T: 我很高兴接受您的申请。您可以到网点领取信用卡申请表格，完整填写，并提供以下三类证明文件：您的本人有效护照复印件以及《外国人居留证》复印件和财力证明；您的《外国人居留证》或"外国人居留许可"的有效期应在 1 年（含）以上，且距到期日应在 1 个月以上。
C: 什么是财力证明？
T: 财力证明包括两种：一种是收入证明，另一种是资产证明。收入证明是指政府机构、企业开具的最近三个月的正式工资单或收入证明，证明上需加盖公司章或财务章原件。而资产证明是指自有房产证明复印件。
C: 信用额度有多少？
T: 我们会根据您所提交的证明材料来审核信用额度的。
C: 那信用卡的利息是如何计算的？
T: 消费透支您可以享受 20 到 50 天的免息期。您只要在对账单提示的到期还款日之前全额还款，消费透支部分可以享受免息期。一旦过了免息期，就要从交易日起，按每天万分之五计算透支息，如果在到期还款日前连最低还款额也没有还入，还要按照最低还款额未还部分的 5% 征收一笔滞纳金。注意，取现透支没有免息期，一旦透支，按每天万分之五计算透支利息。
C: 如何还款？

Credit Card

Applying for a BOC Credit Card

BOC credit card is a double-currency credit card, designed for global use according to international standard. A foreigner living in Beijing is planning to have one. What documents should he provide to the bank? How long will it take to get a new card? How long is the grace period? He has many questions concerning the card. Now a bank clerk at the credit card service center is trying to help him.

T: Teller   C: Customer

T: Hello, this is the Customer Service Center of Bank of China. My name is Catherine. Can I help you?

C: I am a Canadian living in Beijing, and I'd like to know whether I can apply for a credit card issued by Bank of China and how to do that?

T: Of course you can if you meet the following requirements: a job with regular income in Beijing, good working performance and the certificate of the real estate under your name.

C: I think I am OK with all those requirements. But how do I apply?

T: We are glad to accept your application. You can get an application form at a branch of our bank first. Fill out the application form and bring it back with a copy of your passport, your residence certificate and financial certificate. The term of your residence certificate should be no less than one year and the time from current date to the expiration date should be more than one month.

C: What's the financial certificate?

银 行 英 语
Banking English

T: 您可以到柜台还款也可以选择自动还款,在信用卡的到期还款日,银行系统会自动从您在中行的活期一本通账户进行扣款。

C: 卡的有效期多少?

T: 3年。

C: 好的,我知道了。谢谢。

T: 不客气,欢迎您致电中国银行。我们将热忱为您服务。

中国银行股份有限公司北京建国门外支行
Bank of China Limited Beijing Jianguomenwai Subbranch

Credit Card

T: The financial certificate refers to two things: income certificate and asset proof. Your income certificate should be issued by the local government or your employers and it should be for the latest three months; financial stamp or official stamp is needed. Your asset proof refers to a copy of certificate of your own real estate.

C: What about my credit limit?

T: We will set the credit limit on the basis of the materials you provide.

C: If I use the card for shopping, how is the overdraft interest calculated?

T: You can enjoy 20—50 days of interest-free period for your consumption. If you pay the total amount before the payment due date no interest will be charged. But if you don't, we have to charge you interest at the rate of 0.05% per day from the transaction day. If the required minimum amount is not paid before the payment due date, you will be charged 5% of the outstanding part of the minimum amount as penalty. Please note that interest-free period is not applied to cash transaction. Overdraft interest for cash transaction will be charged at the rate of 0.05% per day immediately from the transaction day.

C: How do I make repayment?

T: You can pay the bill over the counter or by auto-payment service, in which case the bank will transfer the money from your current account to your credit card to make a full payment at the due date.

C: How long is the term of the card?

T: 3 years.

C: OK, I've got it. Thanks a lot.

T: My pleasure, thanks for calling Bank of China. I am glad that I could be of some help.

NOTES

1. My pleasure. 不客气。

    同样的意思,也可以说 You are welcome. 或 It's a pleasure. 这两句话一般也都可用于应对他人的感谢之词。而需要注意的是 With pleasure. 的用法。With pleasure. 表达的是某人欣然接受,乐于去做某件事的意思。例如:

    A: Tom, would you please go to the grocery store to get me some wine?

    汤姆,你能去趟食品店帮我买些酒回来吗?

    B: With pleasure.

    当然可以。(十分乐意为您效劳!)

2. 围绕信用卡有许多专门的词组和用法,下面列举的都是在指导客户填写申请表时经常会用到的,我们不但要熟记,更要学会灵活运用。

    金卡:gold card 普通卡:classic card

    个人基本资料:personal details   职业资料:employment information

    对账单地址:billing address/monthly statement address

    联系人:personal reference

    主卡:principle card/master card 附属卡:supplementary card/affiliated card

    自动还款业务:auto-payment service

    全额还款:full payment   最低还款额:minimum payment

    到期还款日:payment due date

3. 关于外籍人申请中银系列信用卡时所需提供的收入证明,除了文中提到的政府或单位开具的工资单是必须提供的材料之外,还有一些材料会帮助审批人员更好地掌握申请人资信状况,例如:

    (1) A copy of the applicant's salary passbook with the depositor's name, bank account number, and the salary entries on it for the latest three months

    银行代发工资的存折复印件(需显示有存款人姓名、账号、最近三个月薪水入账信息)

    (2) A copy of tax-paid certificate for the latest three months

    最近三个月的个人所得税完税证明复印件

    (3) A copy of the payment certificate of social insurance

    社会保险扣缴凭证复印件

    而原文中提到的申请人需要提供的资产证明,除了自有房产证明是必须提供的材料之外,我们还可以建议申请人提供:

    (1) The applicant's driver's license of a motor vehicle 自有机动车行驶证

    (2) A copy of time deposit certificate or a copy of term deposit passbook with the depositor's name, term of deposit and the amount on it. (The period of the

time deposit should be at least one year)

银行定期存款单/存折复印件(需显示存款人姓名、存款年期及金额,要求定期存款存期至少一年)

(3) A copy of current deposit passbook with the depositor's name, bank account number and the balance on it, and the money should be deposited for over three months.

银行活期存款存折复印件(需显示存款人姓名、账号和账户余额,要求开户至少三个月以上)

(4) Copies of purchase certificates of fund, treasury bond, enterprise bond, with the purchaser's name, bank account number and the balance on them.

基金、国债、企业债券购买凭证复印件(需显示购买人姓名、账号和账户余额)

(5) A copy of purchase certificate of commercial insurance, which should have the purchaser's name, the amount insured, and the certificate of paying insurance premiums

购买商业保险证明复印件(需显示购买人姓名、保险金额、缴纳保险费证明)

(6) Copies of member cards which include: golf club member card, China Mobile or China Unicom VIP card, Air China's Platinum companion card, golden card and silver card, Golden Sky Pearl Card of China Southern Air, golden card or silver card of China Eastern Air Club. (The cards should have the applicant's name and the valid period on them.)

会员卡类复印件,包括:高尔夫会籍卡、中国移动、中国联通贵宾卡、国航知音白金卡、金卡、银卡会员卡、南航明珠卡金卡、银卡会员卡、东航万里行俱乐部金卡、银卡会员卡(需显示姓名和卡片有效期)

4. valid 有效 invalid 无效,也叫 null and void

The lapse of time will render the guarantee null and void. 时间的推移会使担保失效。

5. full payment 全额付款 partial payment 部分付款

Banking English

信用卡业务—3

申请长城人民币信用卡

一位客户正在柜台询问办理中银长城人民币信用卡的一般流程。从技术层面讲,长城人民币信用卡是准贷记卡,和一般意义上的信用卡是不同的。让我们来看看银行职员是如何向客户说明它们的不同点的。

T: 柜员　　C: 客户

T: 下午好,您办理什么业务?
C: 是的,我想了解申请信用卡的业务。昨天接到通知,我公司与贵行签定了代发工资协议,我想申请一张中银长城卡作为工资卡,请给我解释一下怎样办理好吗?
T: 首先,您应填写申请表,最重要的就是您的资信状况,包括您的薪水和其他收入。其次,您应提供您护照的复印件一份。您应将所有资料交给贵单位财务或人事部门,由其统一负责与我行接洽,完成后续办卡手续。
C: 申请信用卡需要费用吗?

Applying for a BOC Great Wall Domestic Card

A customer is asking about the procedures of applying for a BOC Great Wall Domestic Card at the counter. Technically, BOC Great Wall Domestic Card is a type of quasi-credit-card, which is different from credit card in general sense. Let us see how the bank clerk explains the difference to the customer in the following conversation.

T: Teller   C: Customer

T: Good afternoon. Can I help you?

C: Yes. I would like to know how to apply for a credit card. I was informed yesterday that our company has signed an agreement with your bank on the payroll account of us employees. And so, I'd like to apply for a Great Wall Domestic Card as my salary card. Can you explain how to get it?

T: First you need to fill in the application form. The most important information is your creditworthiness, such as your current salary and some other reliable sources of income. Second, a copy of your passport is required. When the materials are ready, your need to give the documens to the Financial and HR Department of your company, who will contact us and finish all the follow-up procedures for you.

Banking English

T: 不需要,但需要一次性收取3年年费。
C: 我知道了。
T: 顺便说一下,从技术上来说,中银长城卡是准贷记卡。
C: 什么是准贷记卡?
T: 与普通意义上的信用卡不同,准贷记卡没有免息期,透支利率为日息万分之五,但银行按活期利率给您卡中的余额记息。
C: 哦,正合我意,非常感谢。
T: 别客气。再见!
C: 再见!

NOTES

1. payroll account 工资户　staff payroll account 职工工资户
   e.g. Can you transfer it to his payroll account?
        你能将款打到他的工资折上吗?
        payroll process 代发工资
2. technically speaking 从技术层面上讲。口语交流时,也可简单说成 technically. 类似的表达结构还有:generally speaking, 一般说来;frankly speaking, 坦白讲;strictly speaking, 严格说来。
3. guarantor 担保人　guarantee 被担保人　guaranty 担保

148

Credit Card

C: Is there any charge for that?

T: No charge for just the application part itself, but a lump sum of annual fee for 3 years will be deducted from the card automatically.

C: OK, I see.

T: Oh, by the way, technically speaking, Great Wall Domestic Card is a quasi-credit-card.

C: What is quasi-credit-card?

T: It is different from a credit card in general sense. A quasi-credit-card has no interest-free period and the interest rate, I mean, once you overdraw, is 0.05% per day. But, on the other hand, the bank pays you interest for the money you deposit in your quasi-credit-card. Interest is calculated at the rate of savings account.

C: Oh, I think I am OK with that. Thank you very much.

T: You are welcome. Bye.

C: Bye.

中国银行股份有限公司北京平谷支行
Bank of China Limited Beijing Pinggu Subbranch

信用卡业务—4

信用卡一般取现手续

一位客户正在中国银行的某个支行使用信用卡取钱。信用卡取现交易涉及电话授权和收取手续费等操作要点,让我们来看看柜员是如何向客户解释相关问题的。

 T: 柜员　C: 客户

T: 上午好,请问我能为您做点什么?
C: 上午好,我有一张国际信用卡,想取一些人民币可以吗?
T: 我先看看您的卡好吗?
C: 当然可以。
T: 我行目前只能受理维萨卡、万事达卡、JCB卡、大莱卡、美国运通卡五种信用卡的柜台取现业务。您的维萨卡没问题,要取多少?
C: 我想取1000人民币。
T: 您的卡取现手续费是3%,从您卡中自动扣除,没问题吧?
C: 手续费太多了!没办法,总没有好,取吧。
T: 这是维萨卡和万事达卡全球统一的收费标准。我需要申请授权,请您稍等。
C: 没问题。

Credit Card

Procedures for Cash Withdrawal with a Credit Card

A customer is using his credit card to withdraw cash at a sub-branch of Bank of China. Cash transaction of credit card involves issues like calling the authorization center for approval code and cash withdrawal commission. Let us see how the bank clerk deals with it at the counter.

T: Teller   C: Customer

T: Good morning! What can I do for you?

C: Good morning! I have an international credit card, and can I withdraw some RMB cash from it?

T: Can I have a look at your card first?

C: Sure!

T: Currently, our bank accepts VISA, MASTER, JCB, DINERS club and AMERICAN EXPRESS. Yours is a VISA card, so I guess it is no problem. How much would you like to draw?

C: I want to take out 1,000 RMB.

T: The service charge is 3% of the amount you withdraw, and it is deducted automatically from your card. Is that OK?

C: Oh, that's too much commission! Well, anyway, it's better than nothing. Go ahead.

T: This is worldwide uniform charge standard of VISA and MASTER organizations, I am afraid. OK, Sir, I need to get the authorization from the call center, please wait a moment.

C: No problem.

Banking English

T: 另外,请出示您的护照或国际驾照。(片刻之后)

T: 您的交易可以受理,请您在横线上签字确认,此签字与卡背面的签字应基本一致。

C: 好的。

T: 谢谢,这是您的钱、护照以及水单,如果您想把未用完的人民币再换回外币请保存好水单,在两年之内可以办理退汇手续。

C: 谢谢!再见!

T: 再见!欢迎您再来。

NOTES

1. go ahead 请继续。(可以使用于暂时打断别人说话后请人继续说,或是继续做。)

2. It's better than nothing. 有总比没有好。类似的说法还有:Better late than never. (迟到总比不来的好。)

3. uniform charge 统一费率　flat charge 按笔收费
   The L/C advising fee is a flat charge of USD 24.
   每笔信用证的通知费为 24 美元。

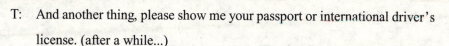

Credit Card

T: And another thing, please show me your passport or international driver's license. (after a while...)

T: I am glad to tell you that your request is approved. Please sign your name on this line and make sure the signature is the same as the one at back of your card.

C: OK.

T: Thank you. Here is your money, passport and exchange memo. By presenting this memo to the bank, you'll exchange the unused RMB back to foreign currency within 2 years.

C: Thank you! Good-bye!

T: Good-bye! Welcome to our bank again.

中国银行股份有限公司国际贸易中心支行

Bank of China Limited Beijing World Trade Centre Subbranch

银行英语
Banking English

信用卡业务—5

外卡取现/授权要求

一位客户正在柜台询问有关外卡取现授权的相关规定。

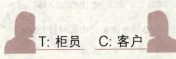

T: 柜员   C: 客户

T: 您好,请问您办理什么业务?
C: 我能用信用卡在这里取现吗?
T: 可以出示一下您的卡吗?
C: 可以,这张可以吗?
T: 对不起,先生,您的这张卡是借记卡,柜台不受理借记卡业务。但是您可以去ATM机取钱。
C: 噢,这张卡可以吗?
T: 是的,这张可以,请出示您的护照。
C: 好,给您。
T: 请问您取多少钱?
C: 1500美元。
T: 请您稍等。
C: 好的,谢谢!
T: 对不起,先生,我们已经与授权中心联系过了,您不能取1500美元。
C: 为什么?
T: 对不起,我们不知道原因。恐怕您只能自己打电话到发卡行查询具体原因。
C: 哦,我想可能是我取得太多了。我可以少取一些吗?

Cash Withdrawal/Authorization Requirements for Foreign Credit Card

A guest is asking a clerk at BOC about cash withdrawal and the authorization requirements.

T: Teller   C: Customer

T: Hello, Sir, is there anything I can do for you?

C: Yes, can I take some money from my credit card here?

T: OK, could you please show me your card?

C: Sure, is this card OK?

T: Sorry, Sir, your card is a debit card, and we don't accept debit card at our counter. But you can try the card on the ATMs.

C: Oh, what about this one?

T: Yes, this one is OK. Please show me your passport.

C: OK, here you are.

T: How much would you like to withdraw?

C: One thousand five hundred US dollars.

T: Please wait a moment.

C: All right, thank you.

T: Sorry Sir, I have just contacted the credit card authorization center and you are not allowed to withdraw $1500.

C: Why?

T: Sorry, we don't know the reason, I am afraid you have to call the issuing bank to cheque the reason yourself.

C: Oh, I think maybe that's too much. What about withdrawing less this time?

Banking English

T: 可以。

C: 请试一下 1200 美元。

T: 对不起,您的请求被拒绝了。

C: 我还可以再试一下更小的金额吗?

T: 可以,不过我们只能给您要最后一次授权了,因为每张卡在我这里每天只能要 3 次授权,现在已经失败两次了。这次如果还无法取出,您只能明天再来了。

C: 哦,那就帮我取 800 美元吧。

T: 授权中心批准了 800 美元。

C: 太好了,非常感谢!

T: 不客气!请您签字。

C: 好。

T: 这是您的护照、信用卡、800 美元和取现单据,请查收。

C: 没问题,谢谢!再见!

T: 欢迎您再次光临!再见!

NOTES

1. Could you please do something : 请您(做)……好吗?(语气委婉的说法)

    e.g. Could you please show me your credit card?

    请您给我看一下您的信用卡,好吗?

2. 围绕信用卡柜台取现,有一组词汇是经常会用到的。例如:to call the credit card authorization center 致电信用卡授权中心,to ask for the approval code 索要授权号码,to contact the issuing bank 与发卡行联系,commission 手续费,(VISA) logo (维萨的)标识,cash withdrawal transaction 取现交易,non-cash transaction 非现金交易等等。

Credit Card

T: OK.

C: Please try $1200.

T: Sorry, your request is denied again.

C: Can I try much less?

T: Yes, but this is the last time for an authorization request, because we are only allowed to place such request three times per day, and now we have failed twice. If it doesn't work this time, you will have to come tomorrow.

C: Oh, please help me withdraw $800.

T: $800 is approved by the authorization center.

C: Great, thank you very much.

T: You are welcome. Please sign your name here.

C: All right.

T: Here is your passport, your credit card, $800, and the voucher, please have a cheque.

C: No problem, thank you! Bye-bye.

T: Welcome to our bank again next time. Bye-bye.

银行英语
Banking English

信用卡业务—6

介绍信用卡的类型功能及费率标准

一位外国客人想办一张由中国银行发行的银行卡。但是他似乎对于我行种类繁多的银行卡有些迷惑。毕竟那些卡的名字、功能以及收费标准都是不同的。现在,一位银行卡中心的销售代表正在为这位客户分别介绍我行银行卡大家族里的每一位成员。

R: 信用卡销售代表　　C: 客户

C: 喂,中国银行吗?
R: 欢迎致电中国银行客服中心,我是兰迪。请问您需要什么帮助?
C: 我想办理中国银行的卡,请帮我介绍一下贵行提供卡的种类和特点好吗?
R: 好的,我们有借记卡和信用卡。您需要哪一种?
C: 我想要一张信用卡。
R: 信用卡有两种:贷记卡和准贷记卡。
C: 它们有什么区别?
R: 贷记卡功能比较多,可以透支消费,可以透支取现。如果是消费刷卡,在到期还款日之前全额还清欠款,是免息的。过了到期还款日,要从交易日起每天收取万分之五的利息。透支取现没有免息,要收每天万分之五的利息。

Credit Card

Introduction to Credit Card—Type, Function and Charge Standards

Unit 6

A foreign guest is hoping to apply for a card of Bank of China. But he seems a bit puzzled about the various types of cards we are offering. The names of the cards are different. The functions are different. And the charges are different too. Now a sales representative at the call center is introducing each member of our big bankcards family to this foreign guest.

 R: Credit Card Sales Representative   **C: Customer**

C: Hello, is that Bank of China?

R: Hello, thanks for calling BOC call center. This is Landy, what can I do for you?

C: I want to apply for a Bank of China card. What kinds of cards do you provide and what are their features?

R: We have debit card and credit card. Which one do you prefer?

C: I think I'll have a credit card.

R: There are two kinds of credit card, standard-credit-card and quasi-credit-card.

C: What are the differences between them?

R: Standard-credit-card has more functions, such as direct consumption and cash overdraft. If you use the card for shopping, you will have a grace period before payment due date. After the due date, however, the interest rate of overdraft is 0.5‰ per day from the transaction day. There is no interest-free-period if you withdraw cash from the card, and the interest rate is 0.5‰ per day.

Banking English

C： 准贷记卡呢？

R： 准贷记卡，没有免息期，一旦透支，按照每天万分之五收取利息。但是，准贷记卡中的存款是计算活期利息的。

C： 您讲得很清楚，谢谢您这么耐心地给我讲解。

R： 别客气，如果还有其他的问题或需要欢迎再次致电。感谢您选择中国银行。

C： 再见！

R： 再见！

NOTES

1. 在日常银行服务中，无论是服务中心还是网点柜台，随时都会接到客户打来的咨询电话，掌握一些必要的接听电话的英语句式和词汇就十分必要了。下面列出的就是经常会用到的一些句子：

   (1) This is Bank of China, may I help you?
   这里是中国银行，有什么可以为您效劳的？
   接电话时最简单的自我介绍的方法就是"This is..."。

   (2) Who is that speaking? 请问您是哪位？
   询问对方是谁的问句有很多，除了上面这句，我们还可以说"Who am I talking to?" "Who am I speaking with?" 以及非常口语化的 "And you are?"等等。

   (3) I'll ask my manager to answer the phone. Just a second.
   我这就去找我们经理来听电话，请稍等。
   还能表达类似意思的较口语化的句子是："I'll put him on the phone, just hang on..." 我让他来听电话，稍等……

   (4) I am afraid he is not here at the moment. Would you please call back later?
   实在抱歉，他现在不在。您可不可以待会儿再打过来？

   (5) May I take your message? 或是 Would you like to leave a message? 你想留言吗？

   (6) please do not hesitate to contact... 径与……联系

Credit Card

C: And what about the quasi-credit-card?

R: It has no interest-free-period. Once it is overdrawn, interest is charged at the rate of 0.5‰ per day. But the bank pays you interest on the amount of your deposit according to savings account rate.

C: Oh, I think I am all clear about that. Thank you for your patient explanation.

R: You're welcome. If you have any other question or need any help, please do not hesitate to call us again. Thank you for choosing Bank of China.

C: Good-bye!

R: Good-bye!

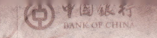

Banking English

信用卡业务—7

自动取款机故障

　　自动取款机发生故障可是一件很让人恼火的事。当取款机无法正常出钞，客户银行卡上的余额却相应减少的时候，客户尤其会感到不满或是焦虑。作为银行职员，怎样去处理这样一些尴尬的场面呢？我们应该如何做才能消除客户的不满，让他们理解并确信其资金的安全性呢？下面就是三个有用的实例。

 T: 柜员　　C: 客户

例1

T: 您好,请问有什么需要帮助的吗？

C: 是的,我刚刚在取款机上取钱,但它只给了我这张纸和卡,没有给我钱,我该怎么办？

T: 请别着急,让我查看一下。
　　(看过回单)是这样的,由于某种原因您的这笔交易没有成功,您看这里标有"失败"。

C: 真的吗？让我看一下。真的,我太着急了没看清楚,对不起。

T: 没关系,很高兴能为您提供帮助。

C: 非常感谢,再见！

T: 不客气,再见！

例2

T: 您好,请问有什么需要帮助的吗？

C: 是的,我刚刚在取款机上取钱,但它只给了我卡,钱还在那个机器里面。没给我钱,一分也没给,我现在该怎么办？

When the ATM is Not Working Properly

ATM breakdown is annoying. People hate it when they try to withdraw some money and the money doesn't come out but it is deducted from his or her account anyway. How to cope with this awkward situation? What proper steps should be taken to let the customers calm down and to assure them of their money safety and timely refund? Here are three examples.

T: Teller   C: Customer

Example One

T: Good morning, Sir, what can I do for you?

C: Oh yes, when I was trying to withdraw some money from that ATM just now, no money came out, and the machine only returned me the card and this receipt, what should I do now?

T: Don't worry, please! Let me cheque it for you immediately. (After looking at the receipt) Oh, I see, it is because your withdrawal transaction just failed for some reason. You see the word "REJECTED" printed here?

C: Really? Let me take a look. Oh yes, you are right, I was too hurried to read it carefully. I am sorry for it.

T: It doesn't matter. I am glad that I could be of help.

C: Thank you very much. Good-bye!

T: You're welcome. Bye!

Example Two

T: Good morning, is there anything I can do for you?

Banking English

T: 请别着急,请给我看看机器出的回单。
C: 对不起,我忘取了。
T: 请稍等,我再帮您去查一下 ATM 的交易记录。相信我,一切都会解决的。(大约三分钟过后……)您的这笔交易没有成功,ATM 的交易记录显示"失败",并没有扣款。
C: 最好是这样!谢谢,再见!
T: 不客气,再见!

例 3

T: 您好,请问有什么需要帮助的吗?
C: 我刚刚在 ATM 上取款,但是没有给我钱。
T: 请让我看一下您的交易回单。
C: 好的,给您。
T: 您的这笔交易没有成功,您看这里标有"失败"。
C: 但是我的账户已经被扣款了。
T: 请稍等,我再帮您去查一下 ATM 的交易记录。
(片刻后)我们的交易记录显示,此笔交易并没有成功,钱也会马上返还到您的账户上。让我来给您解释一下,当您在 ATM 上取款时,ATM 机会向您的银行发出取款信息,那边收到信息后会进行相应操作,接受或拒绝您的请求。在收到发卡行的授权信息以前,ATM 机不会向您提供现金。这个操作是有时间限制的,如果信息传送超时,我们就无法接到付款的信息,ATM 机就会拒绝您的请求,并且不提供现金。但这时您的银行已经从您的账户中扣掉这笔钱了。

Credit Card

C: Oh, yeah, there is I just wanted to get some cash from your ATM, but, here, my card is ejected but my money is still retained in that damn machine. No money, nothing at all! What should I do now?

T: Please don't worry; let me have a look at the transaction receipt, please.

C: What? The receipt? Sorry that I forgot to take it.

T: Please wait a moment; I am going to cheque the transaction record of this ATM for you. Trust me, everything will be just fine. (About three minutes later...) Your last transaction did not succeed, and the record says it was "REJECTED". Your money is still in your card.

C: Well, it better be! Thanks! Good-bye!

T: You are welcome! Good-bye.

Example Three

T: Good morning, May I help you?

C: I tried to withdraw money from the ATM, but it did not give me the money.

T: Please let me take a look at the transaction receipt.

C: OK, here you are.

T: Your last transaction did not succeed. You see, it says "rejected".

C: But the money has been deducted from my account!

T: Please wait a second, I'll cheque the transaction record of this ATM for you. (A moment later) According to the record, your transaction was not successful and the money will soon be returned to your account. Let me explain to you how it works. When you withdrew money from the ATM, the machine sent out a withdrawal request to your card-issuing bank. After receiving the request, the bank will handle it accordingly, that is, either approve the request or disapprove it. The ATMs here are not allowed to pay you until the issuing bank sends back the approval message. However, all these operations should be done within certain

银行英语
Banking English

C: 那我该怎么把钱取回来?
T: 别担心,当银行结账时就会发现这笔错误,这样您的钱就会回到您的卡中了。
C: 我明白了,谢谢您的解释!
T: 别客气,为您服务是我的荣幸,有问题请和我们联系,欢迎下次再来! 再见!
C: 再见!

NOTES

1. 使用银行卡在ATM上进行现金交易,如果交易失败,ATM打印的回单会显示交易失败的原因,所以交易凭条在处理ATM特殊事件时是非常重要的凭证。

2. 关于ATM机的使用,有些英语词汇在回答客户问题时是经常会用到的。下面就是一些最常用的动词词组或句子:

   (1) Insert the card into the machine and enter PIN number. 将卡插入ATM机中,然后输入密码。

   (2) Enter the amount of cash. 输入取现金额。

   (3) Retrieve the card, cash and receipt. 收回银行卡,拿好现金和凭条。

   (4) Choose a transaction type from a menu of options. 从选择菜单中选择交易类型。

   (5) Cancel a transaction. 取消交易。

   还有一些名词词组也很重要,例如:

   (1) improper insertion 卡插入有误

   (2) a damaged stripe 损坏的磁条

   (3) repeated entries of an invalid PIN 重复输入无效密码

   (4) keyboard ATM 机键盘

   (5) transfer transaction and withdrawal transation 转账交易和取款交易

   (6) the dispensing of cash 出钞

Credit Card

time limit. If the machine couldn't receive the approval message from the issuing bank on time, it would reject your request and no cash is dispensed. But at that time, your issuing bank has already deducted the money from your account.

C: Then what can I do to get my money back?

T: Don't worry. The bank will discover the error when it comes to the settlement work of today's transactions, and then, your money will be credited to your account again.

C: OK, I see. Thanks for your explanation.

T: You're welcome. It is my pleasure to offer you some help. If you have any question, please contact me. Welcome to our bank again! Bye-bye!

C: Bye-bye!

信用卡业务—8

处理有争议的取现业务

应对客户的投诉与误解绝非易事。这需要丰富全面的银行业务知识、一些沟通艺术，甚至还需要一点点与生俱来的天分。下面就是两个关于因信用卡交易记录而产生争议的例子，让我们来看看柜员在回答客户问询的时候是如何应对的。

T: 柜员　　C: 客户

例 1

T: 您好。您需要什么帮助吗？
C: 上次我在你的柜台办理了一笔维萨卡的取现业务,但是没有成功您还记得吗？
T: 对不起,您能告诉我是哪一天吗？
C: 大概是周二下午2点左右,我持的是美国花旗银行发行的维萨卡,这是我的卡及护照。
T: 稍等,我查一下。是的,有这笔记录。当时您的卡在POS机上显示通讯故障,我们向授权中心电话索要授权,但对方拒付。
C: 但是我后来给我的银行打电话,对方发现这笔钱已经被中国银行划走了。

Dealing with Complaints and Misunderstandings

> It is always a tough job to deal with customers' complaints and misunderstandings. It requires comprehensive knowledge of banking business, some communication art, and even a bit of genius. Here are two examples of how a teller at the counter replies to customers' complaints and questions about credit card transaction record.

T: Teller   C: Customer

Example One

T: Hello, what can I do for you?

C: I tried to withdraw some money from my VISA card over your counter a few days ago, but failed at that time, do you still remember?

T: Could you please tell me the date?

C: It was about 2 o'clock on Tuesday afternoon, and my VISA card is issued by American Citibank. Here is my card and the passport.

T: OK, please wait for a while, let me cheque it. Yes, there is the record. At that time, the POS machine showed that there was some communication problem, and then we called the authorization center but the transaction was disapproved.

C: But after that I called my bank, only to find that the money had already been subtracted by Bank of China.

Banking English

T: 别着急,我马上帮您查清原因。

(5分钟之后)刚刚我查询了我行的信息科技部,他们从电脑主机上调阅您这笔交易,的确是显示通讯中断,交易未成功。所以中行肯定没有把钱从您的账户上划走。我想当时应该是由于两家银行的通讯中断造成我行没有收到您银行发出的授权号码。

C: 那怎么办?我的钱没了!

T: 您放心,您的钱还在您的账户里,只是您的银行暂时冻结,直到接到维萨组织的清算单才会真正从您账户上划走。如果超过45天未收到清算单,银行会自动把您这笔钱解冻。

C: 可是,我等不了那么久。事情很急!45天啊。

T: 这样,您最好致电您的银行,向其说明情况,您的银行会向中行发出查询,我们会告知交易结果,您的银行收到回复后会尽快解冻您这笔钱的。

C: 如果我让我的银行亲自给您电话,把授权号告诉您可以吗?

T: 恐怕不可以。首先授权号是有时限的;而且,银行索要授权必须通过授权中心,有专门索要授权的途径;另外,您的账户也是由您的发卡行的相关独立信用卡中心根据国际通行惯例来管理的,所以我不能直接与您的银行取得联系。很抱歉。

Credit Card

T: Don't worry, I will find out the reason for you immediately.

(Five minutes later) Just now I called the IT department of our bank, and they traced your transaction back to our host computer system. And they say, according to the computer record, the communication was indeed cut off, and the transaction was aborted. In other words, Bank of China didn't receive the cash withdrawal authorization number from your bank at that time due to communication failure between the two banks and thus it was technically impossible for Bank of China to subtract any money from your account.

C: But what can I do? The money is gone!

T: Don't worry, your money is still in your account. Your bank just had it temporarily frozen until they receive a settlement statement from VISA organization. If they didn't receive any statement after 45 days, they will unfreeze this sum of money automatically.

C: But I can't wait that long. It's an urgency! 45 days is crazy!

T: Well, you can contact your issuing bank and explain the situation. They will send an inquiry letter to us and we will confirm the result of your transaction last time. After our confirmation, your bank will unfreeze your money right away.

C: Can I ask my bank to call you directly, and to tell you the authorization number?

T: I'm afraid not. First, there is a time limit about the use of authorization number; second, the only way you get the number is through the credit card authorization center, that is, we banks have special channel to get the number. Moreover, the management of your account is in the charge of relevant independent credit card center of your bank according to the international practice. So I'm extremely sorry that I can't contact your bank directly.

Banking English

C: 那好吧！谢谢,我会尽快与我的银行联系。
T: 不客气,欢迎您再次光临。
C: 再见！
T: 再见！

例2

T: 您好,请问有什么需要帮助的吗?
C: 我想我的账单有些问题。
T: 请不要着急,是什么问题呢?
C: 上个月我用长城卡在 ATM 中只取了 1000 元现金,但是账单却显示我取了 2000 元,就是又取了 1000 元,可我只取了一次！
T: 您能出示您的账单和护照吗?
C: 给。
T: 是的,这里有两条在同一天取两次现金的记录。请稍等,我给您查一下。
C: 好的,谢谢。
T: 对不起,约翰森先生,我已经核对了您的账户记录和 ATM 日志,没有显示余额错误。两笔的交易时间分别是 16 点 12 分 51 秒和 19 点 30 分 12 秒,地点是中行奥运村支行和王府井支行。您能再好好回想一下您取了几次?
C: 但是我……哦,我想起来了,那天有朋友急需用钱,然后……,我又从 ATM 取了现金。对不起,我是取了两次。非常感谢您的帮助。
T: 别客气！有问题随时可以找我们。再见！
C: 再见！

Credit Card

C: That is all right! I will just talk to them myself. Thanks.

T: You are welcome. Hope to see you again next time!

C: Bye-bye.

T: Bye-bye.

Example Two

T: Good morning. What can I do for you?

C: I think there is something wrong with my monthly statement.

T: Don't worry. What's the problem?

C: Last month I used this Great Wall Card on ATM to withdraw 1000 Yuan only, but the monthly statement shows that I did it twice and I got 2000 Yuan. I didn't do it at all.

T: Oh, would you please show me the statement and your passport?

C: Here you are.

T: Yes, you are right. There are two records for cashing during the same day. I will cheque it immediately, please wait for a while.

C: OK, thank you.

T: Excuse me, Mr. Johnson, I have chequed your account record and the ATM log, and there is nothing wrong with the balance. The transaction time were at 16:12:51 and 19:30:12, and the places were at Olympic Village Sub-Branch and Wangfujing Sub-Branch. Would you please think it over how many times you actually withdrew?

C: But I... Ah, yes, I remember that my friend wanted to borrow some money for emergency that day, and...and then I used the ATM again. Oh, I am sorry. I did it twice. Thank you very much for your help.

T: You are welcome. Please call us if you have any problem. Bye-bye.

C: Bye-bye.

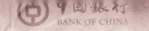

Banking English

NOTES

1. POS machine POS 机，全称为"point-of-sale machine"。
2. 英语中次数的表达是用数词加上"times"来构成的。例如，one time（一次），two times（两次），three times（三次），four times（四次）等等。其中"一次"一般说成"once"，"两次"说成"twice"。
3. international practice 为国际惯例
4. monthly statement=monthly bank statement 银行的月对账单
5. 发卡行 issuing bank
6. 有一些句子在倾听客户意见，处理纠纷时是非常重要的，使用得当，会起到缓和气氛，调节紧张局面的效果，例如：
   (1) Don't worry. Everything will be fine. 别着急，一切都会没事的。
   (2) Would you please tell me what happened? 能不能告诉我发生了什么？

中国银行股份有限公司北京朝阳支行
Bank of China Limited Beijing Chaoyang Subbranch

信用卡业务
Credit Card

(3) Everything is in order. 一切正常。

(4) I hope you don't mind. 希望您别介意。

(5) I am sorry for that. I'll try my best to correct my mistake.
真是很抱歉，我会尽力纠正错误。

(6) Please trust me. 请相信我。

(7) Give me 5 minutes, and I'll give you a satisfactory answer.
请给我 5 分钟时间，我会给您一个满意的答复。

(8) Please wait a second. Our manager is coming to explain it to you.
请稍等，我们的经理马上来为您解释。

(9) Thank you for calling me about this. I'll check it right away. Please hold on for a second and I'll tell you the information.
谢谢您致电提醒我们注意这个问题，我会马上去查，请别挂机，一会儿我给您答复。

(10) Please calm down. I can help you with the problem. Come with me, please.
请冷静一些。我可以帮您解决问题。请跟我来。

(11) I am sorry to hear that. I do apologize for the inconvenience.
抱歉给您带来了这些麻烦，对不起。

(12) I will check with the counter immediately. Please don't be upset, I'll handle this matter.
我马上和柜台人员核实此事，请不要着急生气，您的问题交给我来处理吧。

银行英语
Banking English

信用卡业务—9

ATM 机吞卡的处理

有很多原因会造成自动提款机吞卡。卡磁条损坏,重复输入无效密码,自动提款机通讯故障,以及非法用卡都会造成提款机吞卡。在确认和澄清真实原因之前,我们需要向客户耐心解释并及时有效地处理问题。下面的两个例子就是很好的借鉴。

 T: 柜员　 C: 客户

例 1

T: 您好,请问您要办理什么业务?
C: 您好,我的信用卡被自动提款机吞了,您可以帮我取出吗?
T: 请问您的卡是在哪一台取款机上被吞掉的? 什么时候?
C: 门外的那台,昨天晚上。
T: 好的,可以给我您的护照和自动提款机回单吗?
C: 给您。
T: 请您稍等,我去处理。
C: 好的。
T: 是这张卡吗?
C: 没错,就是这张。
T: 请您在这儿签字……好了,请您收好卡和护照。
C: 非常感谢!
T: 不客气,再见!
C: 再见!

Credit Card

When the Card is Stuck in the ATM

Bankcards are stuck in the ATM for various reasons. A damaged card strip, repeated entries of invalid PIN number, ATM communication failure and illegal use of the card would all be the possible reasons. Before the actual reason is certified or clarified, we need to explain to the customers patiently and handle the issue effectively. Here are two examples of how.

T: Teller   C: Customer

Example One

T: Excuse me, what can I do for you?

C: Hi, my credit card is stuck in the ATM. Could you help me get it out?

T: Your card is stuck in which ATM? And when?

C: Last night in the one outside this branch.

T: OK, would you please show me your passport and the ATM receipt?

C: Here you are.

T: I'll handle it, please wait a moment.

C: OK.

T: Is this your card?

C: Right, it's mine.

T: Sign your name here, please...

   OK, here is your card and passport.

C: Thank you very much.

T: You are welcome. Good-bye.

C: Good-bye.

例2

T: 您好,您需要什么帮助吗?
C: 您好,我的信用卡被门外的ATM吞了,您可以帮我吗?
T: 我看看是什么问题。您稍等,我们需要向信用卡中心要个授权。
C: 好的。
T: (片刻)对不起,经查验这张卡有些问题,我们要收回一段时间。
C: 能有什么问题呢?
T: 这是我们的授权中心和您使用的信用卡发卡组织联系后下达的命令。
C: 好吧。我不用这张卡取钱了。能不能把信用卡给我?
T: 很抱歉。按照国际信用卡组织的惯例对于有问题的卡,要由接受卡的机构收缴,报经发卡组织处理。谢谢您的配合。
C: 只能是这样了。
T: 请出示您的证件。
C: 给您。
T: 请在这里签个字。
C: 谢谢您。您如果需要详细了解卡的情况,请您和您的发卡行联系。
T: 我会的。谢谢!再见!
C: 再见!

NOTES

1. authorization: 授权。各发卡机构(发卡组织或银行)均有授权中心,授权中心掌握着持卡人详细个人资料和交易信息。如代理行(上文提到的接受卡的银行)在受理业务时发现可疑交易,一般通过本行授权中心致电发卡机构授权中心联系,等待发卡机构授权中心的处理意见,并遵照执行。

2. at the disposal of: 处理权在……;由……处理
   at someone's disposal: 由某人处理
   e.g. Credit cards with suspected transactions should be at the disposal of the credit card issuing organization.
   有交易问题的信用卡要报经发卡组织处理。

3. suspicious transaction 可疑交易   large-value transaction 大额交易

Credit Card

Example Two

T: Hello, can I help you?

C: Hi, my card was retained in the ATM outside. Could you help me?

T: Let me see what the problem is. I will call the authorization center, please wait for a while.

C: OK.

T: (A moment later) Sorry, Sir. There is some problem with this card, and our bank will have to keep it for a while.

C: What is the problem?

T: I am afraid this is the order from the authorization center, which has just contacted your card issuing organization.

C: Fine. Then I won't withdraw with this card. Could you return the card to me?

T: Sorry Sir. Cards with suspicious transactions should be kept by the bank and at the disposal of the issuing bank according to the common practice of international credit card organization. Your cooperation will be appreciated.

C: OK. It seems that I have no choice.

T: Would you please show me your passport?

C: Here you are.

T: Please sign here.

C: Thank you. Please contact your issuing bank if you would like to know more about this matter.

T: I will. Thank you. Good-bye.

C: Good-bye.

信用卡业务—10

大堂经理信用卡常识问答

一位外国客人刚刚来到中国,现在,他正在询问大堂经理有关在中国使用信用卡的一些问题。在下面的对话中,你会发现一些有用的信用卡常识方面的英语表达。

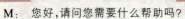

M:大堂经理　G:外宾

M:　您好,请问您需要什么帮助吗?
G:　您好,我是第一次出国,而且就是到你们伟大的国家,我带的信用卡在中国银行怎么使用,我想问问。
M:　谢谢!欢迎您来到我国。我们非常愿意为您服务。您有什么问题,请讲。
G:　我这里有两张卡,需要取现金,请问在这里该用哪张?
M:　我可以看看您的卡吗?
G:　当然可以。给您。
M:　您的两张卡,一张是借记卡,一张是信用卡。
G:　好,你是怎么看出来的?
M:　您看信用卡这张上面有"credit"字样。而这张借记卡是没有的。
G:　它们在使用上有什么区别吗?
M:　信用卡可以在柜台和自助提款机上取款。而借记卡只能在自助提款机取款。
G:　在自助提款机上可以取美元吗?
M:　不行。只能是人民币。取外币必须到营业柜台来。

Credit Card

Questions and Answers about Credit Card

A foreign guest has just come to China, and he is asking the duty manager some questions about credit cards. In the following conversation between them, you will find some useful English expressions concerning some general knowledge about credit cards.

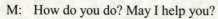

M: Duty Manager   G: Foreign guest

M: How do you do? May I help you?

G: How do you do? It is my first time to go abroad and to come to your great country. I want to know how to use my credit card in your bank?

M: Thank you, welcome to our country. I am glad to help. Would you tell me, exactly, what your problem is?

G: I have two cards here, and I need some cash. Which one can I use here? Or both, maybe?

M: May I have a look at your cards?

G: Sure, here you are.

M: One of your cards is a debit card, and the other one is a credit card.

G: Brilliant! How could you tell?

M: Look, there is the word "credit" on this card, but no such word on the debit card.

G: Is there any difference when I use them?

M: You can use the credit card over the counter here or on the ATMs, but as to the debit card, only ATM use is available.

G: Can I take US dollar cash from the ATMs?

M: I am afraid you can only take RMB from the ATMs. If you want to withdraw foreign currency, you have to come to the bank counter.

Banking English

G: 这是你们银行的长城借记卡,它都有什么功能呢?

M: 好的。您可以在中国或全球带有"银联"标志的自动提款机上进行提款,也可以在存款机办理存款,在可提供该项服务的商场消费,也可以在柜台办理存取款、转账、个人实盘外汇买卖、开放式基金申购等业务。

G: 真不错。那么,这张卡每日能够取多少钱呢?

M: 每日提取限额由您的发卡行制订,是与贵国货币提取额相当的人民币额度。

G: 原来是这样。谢谢您的帮助。我准备取些钱,再到其他城市走走。

M: 您如果时间紧可以从自动取款机取款,但是一次限额是 2500 元人民币。如果您需要更多的现金,您只能在柜台办理,且当日取现不可超过 20,000 元人民币。

G: 我今天先取一些钱,过几天再取。谢谢您。

M: 不客气。再见!

G: 再见!

NOTES

1. available 可获得的,可用的,可看见的

   e.g. Do you have a room available for rent? 你有没有可供租住的房间?

   e.g. I am afraid these shoes are not available in your size.

   对不起,恐怕符合您的尺码的鞋现在没有货了。

   在具体语境中,available 的具体含义会有细微变化,例如下面句子中的 "available" 就表示有空闲,有时间的意思。

   e.g. I think Alice is available this afternoon. You can talk to her about your problem.

   我觉得爱丽丝今天下午应该有空,你可以向她说说你的问题。

2. 关于信用卡和借记卡的区别问题。

   日常柜台服务中,我们会发现不少国外的客人并不真正了解自己手中使用的银行卡究竟是借记卡还是信用卡(贷记卡)。由于借记卡与贷记卡在产品结构、清算方式、适用规定以及功能等方面都有着巨大差别,我们在柜台有时就需要较为细致地解释二者之间的区别,这样才能相应地提供令客户满意的金融服务,下面就是我们在面对客户时可能经常会谈论到的借记卡和信用卡的不同点,细看之下我们就会发现,同样的意思,我们可以用不同的词语来表达:

   (1) Debit cards don't have a credit card company logo on them; instead, they just have the name of the issuing bank, the account number and the card holder's name sometimes.

   信用卡的卡面上会有信用卡公司的特有标识,而借记卡则没有。借记卡上通常只会体现发卡行名称、卡号(账号),有时还会有持卡人姓名。

Credit Card

G: There is this Great Wall debit card of your bank. What functions does it have?

M: OK, first, you can use the card to withdraw money from all the ATMs with this logo of "China UnionPay" in China and around the world. Second, you can deposit money into this card through the CDMs. Third, you can go shopping with this card. Moreover, by using this card, you can make such personal finance transactions as cash deposit and withdrawal, money transfer, personal foreign exchange trade and open-ended funds management over the bank counters.

G: That's good. Well, how much money can I take from the card each day?

M: The limit is set by the issuing bank, and normally, it is the equal amount in RMB to that in your home currency.

G: I see, thank you for your help. I want to take out some money and have a visit to other cities.

M: If you are in a hurry, you can draw money from the ATMs, but the limit is 2,500 Yuan each time and the total amount you withdraw from the ATMs should not exceed 20,000 Yuan per day. If you need more cash, you have to go to the counter and queue for your turn.

G: No problem! I will take some money today and draw again after a few days. Thank you.

M: You are welcome, see you.

G: See you.

Banking English

(2) When you use your debit card to make a purchase, it's just like using cash. Your debit card is usually attached to a chequeing account or a current account, which is automatically debited when you use your debit card to buy things. That is, the cost of your purchase is deducted from the funds you have in that account.

使用借记卡消费的时候,就如同使用现金消费。你的借记卡通常会和你的支票账户或是活期账户勾连,当你刷借记卡消费时,账户里的钱会自动扣除。

(3) When you use your credit card to make a purchase, you are using someone else's money, specifically the issuer of the credit card or the issuing bank.

当你使用贷记卡消费时,你实际上是在使用别人的钱。具体说来,就是信用卡发卡机构或是发卡行。

(4) While a credit card is a way to "buy now, pay later," a debit card is a way to "pay now, buy later".

如果说信用卡是"先消费,后存款"的话,那么借记卡就是"先存款,后消费"。

中国银行股份有限公司北京海淀支行
Bank of China Limited Beijing Haidian Subbranch

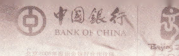

信用卡业务
Credit Card

Exercise

I. Fill in the blank

1. The debit card is not accepted in counter, and you can use the ATM to _____ money.
   柜台不接受借记卡业务,您可以通过自动取款机取现。

2. I am not _____ _____ the credit card business, could you give me some _____?
   我对贷记卡业务不熟悉,能给我讲解一下吗?

3. The merchant also has to ask the customer to sign the sales slip and _____ the signature on the sales slip _____ that on the back of the card.
   商户也会要求客户在签购单上签名,并与卡背后的签名核对。

4. We should never _____ the customers' request.
   我们从来不拒绝客户的需求。

5. The transaction commission has been _____ from your account.
   交易手续费已经从您的账户扣除了。

6. _____ _____ your accent, you must be from Great Britain.
   根据你的口音,你一定来自英国。

7. You should turn to your _____ _____ if you forget the password of your credit card.
   如果您忘记了信用卡的密码,您必须到开户行解决。

8. Don't worry, let me _____ it for you.
   别担心,让我来帮您解决。

9. Please _____ me directly when you have troubles.
   当您遇到麻烦时,请直接联系我。

10. A: I'd like to _____ _____ a credit card _____ by Bank of China.
    B: No problem, our _____ _____ _____ _____ is a good choice for you.
    A: 我想申请一张中国银行发行的信用卡。
    B: 没问题,长城国际信用卡可以满足您的要求。

11. According to business _____, pleasc show me your passport.
    根据业务规定,请出示您的护照。

12. Please change your _____ _____ _____.
    请您更改您的初始密码。

13. _____ _____ is 20 Yuan per year.
    年费是每年 20 元。

14. We will grant you a credit limit according to your _____ _____.
    我们将根据您的月收入给您核定信用额度。

Banking English

15. You are required to provide some _____ _____.
    您需要提供一些个人信息。

16. If you do not want to make a deposit, you have to find a _____.
    如果您不想存入保证金，就需要找担保人。

17. Can I _____ _____ _____ at your card first?
    我能先看看您的卡吗？

18. It'll be _____ from your card.
    它将从您的卡中自动扣除。

19. We have to get the _____ _____ first.
    我们要先取得授权号码。

20. What are the differences _____ credit card and debit card?
    信用卡与借记卡的区别有哪些呢？

II. Translation

1. 在到期日，本金和产生的利息会自动转存。
   _____

2. 您的信用额度是您每月可以使用的最大金额。
   _____

3. 我们将根据透支的金额、利率和天数计算透支的利息。
   _____

4. 您的婚姻状况会影响您的信用额度。
   _____

第六部分 银行保管箱业务
Part VI Safe Deposit Box

Banking English

保管箱业务—1

介绍开办保管箱业务的分支机构

史密斯先生是一名前来参加奥运会的运动员。现在,他正在我行某网点询问我行保险箱业务的相关问题。

M: 大堂经理　C: 客户

M: 您好！您看来非常高兴,您需要什么帮助吗？
C: 我非常幸运,得了一枚金牌。我还要在中国待一段时间。你们能代我保管这枚奖牌吗？
M: 祝贺您获了奖牌。不过,我们这里没有这项业务。建议您到我们开办了保管箱业务的网点办理这项业务。
C: 那也可以,它们在哪？
M: 中银大厦支行、东城支行营业室、奥运村支行开办了这项业务。从这里到中银大厦支行很方便。它就在西单中国银行总行大楼里。
C: 如何走呢？

中国银行股份有限公司北京中银大厦支行
Bank of China Limited Beijing Zhongyin Building Subbranch

Directing Clients to the Right Bank

Mr. Smith is an athlete taking part in the 2008 Olympic Games. Now he is asking a clerk at one of our branches about our safe deposit box service.

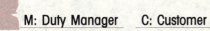

M: Duty Manager   C: Customer

M: Good morning, Sir. You look very happy today. Is there anything I can do for you?

C: Oh, what a lucky person I am! You see, I have won a gold medal! Well, I am still going to be here for a while, so would you please take care of this medal for me?

M: Congratulations on your great performance. But I am afraid we do not have a safe deposit box service here. You can go to some of our sub-branches to do it.

C: That is OK, but where are they?

M: Currently, three Sub-Branches of our bank have the safe deposit box service, and they are: Zhong Yin Da Sha Sub-Branch, Dong Cheng Sub-Branch, and Olympic Village Sub-Branch. Zhong Yin Da Sha Sub-Branch is just located at the head office of Bank of China at Xi Dan, and it is quite convenient for you to get there from here.

C: How can I get there then?

---

medal /'medl/ n. 奖牌, 勋章
take care of 照料, 保管
congratulation /kən,grætʃu'leɪʃən/ n. 祝贺, 恭喜
performance /pə'fɔːməns/ n. 成绩, 表现
safe deposit box 保管箱
convenient /kən'viːnjənt/ adj. 方便的, 合宜的

银行英语
Banking English

M: 您出大门向北走,第一个路口向东再走约100多米,有一个路口,再向北走,一直走到东西走向的大街上,可以乘1路、4路等公交车,到西单下车,西单的西北路口就是。

C: 看来路还很远哪?

M: 路虽然远些,但您如果乘坐出租车,还是很方便的。北京的的士都会热情周到地接待您的。

C: 这倒是好办法。谢谢您!

M: 不客气,再见!

C: 再见!

NOTES

1. congratulations on 祝贺
    e.g. Congratulations on your great performance. 祝贺您取得了好成绩。
    Congratulations on your gold medal. 祝贺您获得了金牌。

2. be located at... 位于……坐落在……
    e.g. Zhong Yin Da Sha sub-branch is just located inside the Head Office of Bank of China at Xi Dan.
    中银大厦支行就在西单中国银行总行大楼里。

3. take a taxi/call a taxi 叫出租车,打的
    e.g. You can also call a taxi. 您也可以乘的士。

4. 在英语中,问路与指路的表达方式很多,有许多习惯的表达法。其中,最基础的是方位词,例如:east 东、south 南、west 西、north 北、northeast 东北、southeast 东南、southwest 西南、northwest 西北、left 左、right 右、here 这儿、there 那儿、front 前方、back 后方、side 侧旁、before... 之前、after... 之后。同时,不同的方位词在句中使用的动词、介词搭配不尽相同,下列例句都是问路与指路中常用的句型,在实际对话中,我们需要灵活掌握:

- Take the one-way street/this road. 走这条单行道/这条路。
- Go along/down the road till you reach the first crossing.
    沿着这条路一直走,直到第一个十字路口。
- Take a left/right. 向左/右转。
- You will see the bank on your left. 在您的左手边您会看到那家银行。
- Keep going 50 meters before you come to a fork road.
    继续走50米,直到您走到一个三叉路口。
- About 100 meters down the road there is another crossing.
    第一个路口向东再走约100多米,有一个路口。
- The bank is just across the street of the hospital.
    银行就在医院的正对面。

Safe Deposit Box

M: Starting from our front gate, go north till you reach the first intersection, then turn east, about 100 meters down the road there is another intersection, and you just turn north again until you reach the main road that goes east to the west. You can take the No.1 or the No.4 bus along the main road to get to Xi Dan, and the head office is right at the northwest corner of Xi Dan intersection.

C: But that sounds pretty far, far away?

M: It is not very close, but it is convenient to take a taxi to get there. I am sure you will receive warm welcome and quality service from one of the taxi driver of our city.

C: That is a good idea. Thank you very much.

M: You are welcome, Good-bye!

C: Bye!

quality /ˈkwɔliti/ *adj.* 优质的
intersection /ˌintəːˈsekʃən/ *n.* 交插路口

中国银行股份有限公司北京知春路支行
Bank of China Limited Beijing Zhicunlu Subbranch

Banking English

保管箱业务—2

在中银大厦支行开立保管箱

史密斯先生来到了中银大厦支行,他想在这里开立自己的保险箱。

T: 柜员　　C: 客户

T: 您好,有什么可以帮助您的吗?
C: 听说这里可以办理保管箱业务,是吗?
T: 是的。您需要吗?
C: 我有一块奖牌需要保管,可以吗?
T: 祝贺您获得了奖牌。如果您办理保管箱业务,您带了有效证件了吗?
C: 带了。您看。
T: 是的,请您先选好箱型,那边有样箱您可以看一下。我们有八种箱型供您选择,不同的箱型收费不同。
C: 我想租一个 A 型箱。
T: A 型箱的位置都比较高,需要用到梯子,没有关系吧?
C: 没有关系。

Opening a Safe Deposit Box at Zhong Yin Da Sha Sub-Branch

Mr. Smith comes to the Zhong Yin Da Sha sub-branch, and he wants to open a safe deposit box there.

T: Teller   C: Customer

T: Good morning, Sir, what can I do for you?

C: I was told that the business of renting a safe deposit box is handled over here. Is that right?

T: Yes, would you like to rent one?

C: Yes. I want to store my medal here in the box while I am in Beijing. Is that OK?

T: Congratulations on your medal. We need your passport to open a safe deposit box for you. Have you got it?

C: Yes. Here you are.

T: Thanks. First of all, please choose the type of your box. You can take a look at the sample boxes over there. We provide altogether eight types of safe deposit boxes and their rental fees are different.

C: I would like to rent a box of type A.

T: Well, most A boxes are located higher on the wall and you'll have to use a ladder to reach them. Is that OK with you?

C: It's OK.

> handle /'hændl/ vt. 处理,操作
> rent /rent/ vt. 租,租赁
> rental /'rentl/ n. 租金
> ladder /'lædə/ n. 梯子

银行英语
Banking English

T: 好的。这是租用保管箱的合约,您先仔细阅读每项条款,没有问题的话请您在这里填写您的个人基本资料,并在最下面签字。合约一式两份,双方各保留一份。"A"型箱有月租方式,比较适用短期使用的客户。用租金为20元,保证金是200元,另外,想向您说明保证金部分将不计利息,保证金在合同期满将全额退还,以上两项共计220元。如果一个月期限太短,可到期办理续租。

C: 没问题,填好了。

T: 谢谢!如果您不介意的话,现在给您注册指纹,一共采三次指样,以便确保我们取得最清晰的一个。好了,注册完成。请您在电脑指纹仪上再试一下刚才注册的指纹,如果电脑不能识别您的指纹,我们会给您重新注册。好了,没问题,给您,这是合约和租金保证金收据。

这是您的保管箱的两把钥匙,您检查一下,没问题的话我给您启封。

好了,给您。钥匙您一定要保管好,如果丢失一把,您需要赔偿200元做一把新的。如果两把都丢失您就需要办理挂失手续,交纳挂失手续费10元,另外还要收取一套新锁和两把钥匙的工本费及凿箱费共800元。所以再次提醒您一定保管好您的钥匙。

中国银行股份有限公司北京三里屯支行
Bank of China Limited Beijing Sanlitun Subbranch

银行保管箱业务
Safe Deposit Box

T: Fine. Here is the lease agreement for renting the safe deposit box. Please read those terms carefully first, fill in your personal information here and then sign at the bottom. The lease agreement is in duplicate, with each party holding one of them having the same effect. The rental fee for an "A" box is 20 RMB per month and it is suitable for short-term use. Besides, you'll have to pay another 200 RMB in advance as a guarantee deposit. I would like you to know that the guarantee deposit does not bear any interest and that it is refundable upon termination of the lease agreement. So altogether, that's 220 RMB. If one month is too short, you can come back and extend the lease term.

C: No problem...Well, it's all done!

T: Thank you! Now, if you don't mind, please allow me to have your fingerprint registered. I'll scan your fingerprint three times to make sure that we get the clearest one...OK, the computer has recorded your fingerprint pattern. Please have a try with your finger on this fingerprint reader. If your fingerprint cannot be identified by the computer, we'll register again...OK, no problem. Here is one copy of the lease agreement as well as a receipt for the rental fees and the guarantee deposit.

Here are the two keys to your safe deposit box shrink-wrapped. Please check them first and if there is no problem, I'll open the plastic package for you.

OK, here you are. Please keep the keys. If one key is lost, you'll have to pay 200 RMB to make a new one. And if you lose both keys, you'll have to report the loss of your keys, and there is a 10 RMB charge for the procedure. And then, you'll have to pay 800 RMB to drill open the box and to change a new lock with two new keys.

lease agreement /liːs əˈɡriːmənt/ n. 租约，租赁协议
term /tɜːm/ n. 条款
guarantee deposit /ˌɡærənˈtiː dɪˈpɒzɪt/ 保证金
refundable /rɪˈfʌndəbl/ adj. 可偿还的，可退还的
termination /ˌtɜːmɪˈneɪʃən/ n. 终点，结束
fingerprint /ˈfɪŋɡəˌprɪnt/ n. 指纹
register /ˈredʒɪstə/ vt. 注册
scan /skæn/ vt. 扫描
identify /aɪˈdentɪfaɪ/ vt. 识别，确定

C: 好，我会的。
T: 请跟我来。
这就是您的箱子，箱号是 717。
C: 我很喜欢这个号码。
T: 这是您箱子上的指纹锁。下次您来的时候，您要先在外面前台的电脑指纹仪上扫瞄指纹，这把锁就会自动打开。然后您进来用我刚才给您的钥匙将保险箱的机械锁打开。一个小时之内您可以打开机械锁两次，但两次开启之间要间隔 30 秒。
C: 谢谢您的帮助。
T: 不客气。下次您自己就可以操作了。再见！
C: 再见！

NOTES

1. have a try 试一下
   e.g. Please have a try with your finger on this fingerprint reader.
   请您在指纹识别器上用手指试一下指纹。

2. in advance 提前，预先
   e.g. You'll have to pay another refundable 200 RMB in advance as the guarantee deposit.
   此外，你需要预先缴纳 200 元作为保证金。

3. position *n.* 位置，地位，身份
   (在金融英语中，position 有时会作"头寸"讲，例如，exchange position 外汇头寸，long position 多头，short position 空头 take a position 开启头寸）
   　　　　vt. 安置，放置
   e.g. Most type A boxes are positioned high up on the wall.
   大多数 A 型箱的位置都比较高。

Safe Deposit Box

C: OK, I will.

T: Please follow me!

This is your box, and the box No. is 717.

C: Oh, I like this number.

T: This is the fingerprint lock of your box. Next time when you come, you first scan your fingerprint at the fingerprint reader outside at the counter, and the lock can be opened by itself. And then, you come in here and use the key I gave you just now to open the metal lock here. You are able to open the metal lock twice within one hour and there should be a 30-second interval between the two openings.

C: Thanks for your help.

T: Not at all. You can do it yourself next time then. Good-bye!

C: Good-bye.

interval /'ɪntəvəl/ n. (时间上的)间隔

中国银行股份有限公司北京佳程广场支行
Bank of China Limited Beijing Jiachengguangchang Subbranch

银行英语
Banking English

保管箱业务—3

开箱及续租

成功开立了自己的保险箱之后，史密斯先生打算试着使用一下保险箱，让我们来看一下他和柜员之间关于开箱的对话。

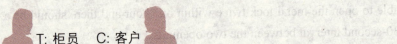

T: 柜员　C: 客户

T: 您好，请问您需要什么帮助吗？
C: 您好，我想开一下箱子。
T: 请告诉我您的箱号。
C: 717。
T: 您贵姓？
C: 史密斯。
T: 我们先核对一下您的指纹，好吗？
T: 没问题，请进。

史密斯先生要在中国继续住上一段时间，所以他打算继续租用保险箱。现在，他正在询问柜员有关保管箱续租的规定。

T: 柜员　C: 客户

T: 您好，您需要帮助吗？
C: 您好，我可以续签租用保管箱的合约吗？
T: 当然可以。您带合约、保证金单据及本人护照了吗？

Safe Deposit Box

Opening a Box and Extending the Lease

After renting a safe deposit box of his own, Mr. Smith decides to use his box this time. Now let us take a look at the conversation between him and the teller about opening the box.

T: Teller   C: Customer

T: Good morning! How can I help you?
C: Oh, hi. I would like to open my safe deposit box.
T: Please tell me the number of your box.
C: 717.
T: And what's your surname, please?
C: Smith.
T: Now please have your fingerprint scanned here, OK?
T: No problem. Please come in.

Mr. Smith decides to stay in China for a while, and thus he wants to extend the lease of his safe deposit box. Now he is asking a teller about relevant regulations about lease extension.

T: Teller   C: Customer

T: Good morning, Sir. Can I help you?
C: Good morning. Can I renew my box lease agreement with your bank here?
T: Yes, of course! Have you got your passport, the initial lease agreement and the receipt of the guarantee deposit?

surname /ˈsɜːneɪm/ n. 姓
renew /rɪˈnjuː/ vt. 更新，继续
initial /ɪˈnɪʃəl/ adj. 首先的，最初的

Banking English

C：这是我的护照,合约和单据在保管箱里呢。
T：好,您录一下指纹,可以了,请进,请把合约和保证金单据拿出来。
C：给您。
T：您再续多长时间?
C：时间长了有优惠吗?
T：有,两年打 9.5 折,三年打 9 折,四年打 8.5 折,五年打 8 折,租五年最合算。租期越长,折扣越多。
C：那再续五年吧。
T：好的,稍等一下,我给您更新一下您在我们电脑里的个人信息。请交 800 元租金……好了,这是您的新合约和相关收据,您收好,建议您放在箱子里。
C：谢谢!
T：不客气。

NOTES

1. to suggest that... 建议某人做某事

   e.g. I suggest that you put them all in your safe deposit box. 我建议您将它们都放在您的保险箱中。(suggest 意为建议,通常在其后面的由 that 引导的从句中的动词应为原型,如例句中的 put 就是用的原型)再请看下面的例句,特别注意 suggest 从句后使用动词原型的格式应为 suggest+that+某人+动词原型：

   e.g. The doctor suggested that I come again next day.
   医生建议我第二天再来。(此句中的 come 就是动词原型)

2. The longer you rent, the more discount you get. 租期越长,折扣越多。中文中"越……越……"的意思在英语中通过连用形容词比较级的形式来表达,类似的表达在前面的单元中也有涉及,请看例句：

   e.g. The more exercise you take, the healthier you will be.
   你越多做锻炼,身体就会越好。

3. 英语说打折的习惯跟中文正好相反,如中文的九折,英文就是 10% discount,中文的八五折,英文就是 15% discount。

Safe Deposit Box

C: Well, here is my passport, and the rest documents are all in my box.

T: OK, then please scan your fingerprint here first....OK, please come inside and get those documents I mentioned.

C: Here they are.

T: How long would you like to extend your lease?

C: Is there any discount for longer lease?

T: Sure! It's 5% for a two-year lease, 10% for three years, 15% for four years and 20% for five years. The longer you rent, the more discount you get.

C: OK, then I'll have an extension of 5 years.

T: Very well, Sir! Please wait a second. I'll update some of your information in our computer and please give me the rental of 800 RMB...OK, finished! Here you are, your new lease agreement plus relevant receipts. Please keep them and I suggest that you put them all in your box.

C: Thanks!

T: You are welcome!

document /'dɒkjʊmənt/ *n.* 文件,单据
extend /ɪks'tend/ *vt.* 延长,伸展,扩大
extension /ɪks'tenʃən/ *n.* 延长(extend 的名词形式)
relevant /'relɪvənt/ *adj.* 相关的,有关联的
suggest /sə'dʒest/ *vt.* 建议

保管箱业务—4

挂失及解挂

史密斯先生不小心将保险箱的钥匙丢失了,他要怎么做才能重新使用保险箱呢?

T: 柜员　　C: 客户

T: 您好,有什么可以帮助您的吗?
C: 我保管箱的钥匙丢了。
T: 那您要办理挂失,请问您带身份证了吗?
C: 带了,我需要怎么办理?
T: 请您填写一下挂失申请书,我们将把您的箱子冻结7天,7天内不会允许任何人开箱,7天后我们将为您办理解除冻结手续,并为您补发一套新钥匙。
C: 我填好了,还有什么吗?
T: 请稍等,我要核实一下您在我们电脑里注册的护照号。好了,没问题了。请您交挂失手续费10元,一套钥匙的工本费及凿箱费共800元。
C: 谢谢,请您收钱。
T: 谢谢。顺便说一下,请保存好这张申请表。下次来办理解除挂失手续时,带上您的挂失申请书和您的证件好吗?
C: 好的,多谢。非常感激您的帮助。
T: 不客气。再见!
C: 再见!

Safe Deposit Box

Reporting Loss and Replacing the Keys

Mr. Smith lost the keys to his safe deposit box. What should he do to use the box again?

T: Teller   C: Customer

T: Good afternoon, Sir! Is there anything I can do for you?

C: Yes. I lost the keys to my box.

T: Well, then you have to report the loss of your keys. Do you have your passport?

C: Yes, here you are. What should I do next?

T: Please fill in this application form for loss report. We are going to have your box sealed for 7 days. You can come back in 7 days to unseal the box and get a new set of keys.

C: OK, I've finished it. Anything else that I need to do?

T: Please wait a moment. I am going to check your registered passport number in our computer first. OK, no problem. ...Now, please give me 10 RMB as the service charge and 800 RMB as the cost of making new keys and drilling open the box.

C: OK, thanks. Here is the money.

T: Thanks. By the way, please keep this application form. Next time when you come to unseal the box, do remember to bring your passport together with this form, OK?

C: OK, thanks a lot. I appreciate your help!

T: It is my pleasure. Good-bye!

C: Bye!

---

seal /siːl/ vt. 封存,加封,密闭
appreciate /əˈpriːʃieɪt/ vt. 感谢,欣赏

Banking English

7天后,史密斯先生前来办理解挂手续。

T: 您好!
C: 您好,前几天我办理了钥匙挂失,今天可以拿到新的钥匙吗?
T: 您的证件和挂失申请书都带了吗?
C: 带了,给你。
T: 没问题,您今天可以拿到新钥匙。
T: 这是您的两把新钥匙,请您妥善保管。
C: 好的,谢谢!
T: 请您在这里签字。好了,谢谢。再见!
C: 再见!

NOTES

1. to report the loss of 报失……,挂失……

   e.g. Well, then you have to report the loss of your keys.
   那您要办理钥匙挂失。

2. 除了对话中的相关句型外,挂失业务还有一些固定且常用的习惯表达,在实际对话中,我们需要灵活掌握,例如:

- loss reporting procedures 挂失程序

  procedures 指办某事需要走的程序,例如: It normally takes X days to complete the procedures of credit card application approval.
  信用卡申请的批准程序一般需要 X 天。

- deposit certificate loss reporting 存单挂失

- the original depository bank 原开户行

- interim loss reporting / formal loss reporting 临时挂失/正式挂失

银行保管箱业务
Safe Deposit Box

After seven days, Mr. Smith comes to our bank to unseal the box.

T: Good morning, Sir!
C: Good morning. Um...I reported the loss of my keys a few days ago. Can I get a new set of keys today?
T: May I have your passport and your Loss Report application form, please?
C: Sure. Here you are.
T: OK, no problem, you can have your new keys today.
T: Here you are: two keys to your box.
C: OK, thanks!
T: Would you please sign here?...OK, thanks! Good-bye!
C: Good-bye!

中国银行股份有限公司北京王府井支行
Bank of China Limited Beijing Wangfujing Subbranch

银行英语
Banking English

保管箱业务—5

退箱

奥运会结束了，史密斯先生要回国了。他打算将保险箱退还银行。请看他和柜员的对话。

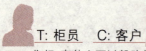

T：柜员   C：客户

T： 您好，有什么可以帮助您的吗？
C： 奥运会结束了。我想把保管箱退掉，取出奖牌，让我的家人分享我的快乐。
T： 太好了！我相信您的亲人都会为您高兴的。您的合约、保证金收据及证件都带了吗？还有两把钥匙？
C： 我的合约在箱子里，我先进去取一下吧。
T： 好吧，您先来验证一下指纹，好的，通过了，请进。
C： 我拿到了。
T： 麻烦您填一下退箱申请书，还有您的两把钥匙给我们，我们再去检查一下您的箱子，只是例行公事，请稍等……请出示一下您的证件，我为您核对一下您填写的申请表。

Returning the Safe Deposit Box

The Olympic Games are over and Mr. Smith is going back. He decides to return the box to the bank. Please look at the conversation between him and one teller.

T: Teller C: Customer

T: Hello, Sir! What can I do for you?

C: The Olympic Games are over. I'd like to return the safe deposit box and take my medal out. I want to share my happiness with my family.

T: That's great! I believe your family will be very happy for you. Did you bring the contract, the receipt of guarantee fee and your identity certificate with you? And the two keys as well?

C: Sure, my contract is in the box. I'll get it first.

T: Well, please check your fingerprint here.... Great, it's accepted. Come in, please.

C: I got it.

T: Please fill out the application form for returning the box and then give the two keys to us. We will check your safe deposit box again, just routine, please wait a second. ...OK! Now, please give me your passport, and I'll go through the filled application form.

---

take sth. out 把某物取出来

family /'fæmili/ n. 可以表示"家庭"这个整体概念；也可以表示"家庭成员"的意思,当解释为"家庭成员"时,单数形式表示复数的意思。

receipt /rɪ'siːt/ n. 收据,收条

identity certificate n. 身份证

as well 也,还有

fingerprint /'fɪŋɡəˌprɪnt/ n. 指纹

Banking English

T: 没有问题,这是您的保证金200元。您的保证金收据我们就收回了。

C: 给您。

T: 好了,您的手续办好了。欢迎您下次再来北京,祝您获得更多的奖牌。

C: 感谢您的祝愿。再见!

T: 再见!

NOTES

1. 本文中用 I got it.表示"我拿到了。"实际上,I got it 的用途很广泛、很口语化,大多表示"我完成了,我达到了"的语境都可以用这个短句。如:

   A: Do you understand the procedure of opening an account?
   你明白开立账户的程序了吗?

   B: I got it.
   我明白了。

2. Well done.与 I got it.类似,口语中用途也很广泛。主要表示"没有问题,做得很好,真棒"的意思。如:

   A: Madam, can you cheque the application form for opening a savings account for me?
   女士,你可以帮我核对这份开户申请书吗?

   B: Well done, I'll open it for you.
   填得很好,我现在为您开户。

   又如:

   A: Mum, I am champion in the ping pong games!
   妈妈,我在乒乓球比赛中拿了冠军!

   B: Oh, really? Well done!
   哦,真的啊?你真棒!

3. guarantee deposit 中的 deposit 指押金,保证金,deposit 一般指存款。

Safe Deposit Box

T: Well done. Here is the guarantee deposit of 200 Yuan for you, and we will keep the receipt for it.

C: Here you are.

T: Thanks. Now, it's all done. Welcome to Beijing next time, and wish you win more medals in the future.

C: Thanks for your wishes. Good-bye!

T: Good-bye!

保管箱业务—6

全自动保管箱业务手续

格林先生想要在奥运村支行开立全自动保险箱业务,他要怎么做呢?

T: 柜员　　C: 客户

T: 您好,我能为您做什么吗?

C: 您好,您这里有保管箱业务吗?

T: 有,我们这里有全自动保管箱业务。您租箱后可以在任意时间,全天24小时,无需银行人员陪同就可以使用到我们提供的保管箱。这款保管箱的特点是私密性比较强。

C: 我如何办理手续?

T: 请您出示护照,填写好一式两份的保管箱租用合约及保管箱租赁申请表一份。

C: 我应该填写哪些内容?

T: 填写您目前的住址、邮政编码及联系电话,现居住酒店名称。另外,您必须向银行提交护照复印件。

C: 好。顺便问一下,租用费是什么标准?

T: 我们这里只有一种箱型,尺寸是390mm×230mm×45mm,年租金为800元,还需要交纳保证金1600元,保证金不计息,在销户时全额退还。

C: 如果我不小心丢失钥匙怎么办?

Safe Deposit Box

Automatic Safe Deposit Box Services in Bank of China

Mr. Green wants to open an auto-safe deposit box in the Olympic Village sub-branch of our bank. What should he do?

T: Teller C: Customer

T: Good morning! What can I do for you?

C: Good morning! Do you provide safe deposit box service here?

T: Yes, we do. And it is auto-safe deposit box. That is to say, when you hire an auto-box, you can use it any time, 24 hours a day, without being accompanied by a teller. With this type of safe deposit box, your privacy can be very well protected.

C: How can I hire it?

T: Please show me your passport, sign the lease agreement here in duplicate and fill out an application form for hiring a box.

C: How should I fill it out?

T: Please write down your present address, postcode, telephone number, and the name of your hotel. Additionally, you should leave us a copy of your passport.

C: OK, I see. By the way, how much is the service charge?

T: There is only one size of the box, which is 45mm×230mm×390mm. And the annual rental of the box is 800 Yuan. Besides, 1600 Yuan should be deposited as the guarantee fee. The guarantee fee doesn't generate interest, but it is fully refundable when you return the box.

C: What should I do if I lose the key?

---

accompany /əˈkʌmpəni/ vt. 陪伴,陪同
present /ˈprezənt/ adj. 现在的,出席的,当前的

Banking English

T: 合同包含涉及钥匙丢失的条款。承租人必须为丢失一把钥匙赔偿400元人民币，两把800元。因此我们提醒您务必保管好钥匙，否则我们除凿开保管箱并提供新钥匙以外，没有其他办法。

C: 知道了，我办理完这些手续后，该怎样使用保管箱呢？

T: 很简单，注册完成后，我们会给您一张进门卡。您下次来的时候，只要刷进门卡后输入您预留的四位密码；然后，屏幕上的信息将引导您进入放置箱子的房间；这样您就可以将箱子取出并带到整理室；最后，您使用钥匙开箱就行了。

C: 明白了，谢谢，再见！

T: 很高兴为您服务，再见！

NOTES

1. OK/Well, I see. 好的，我知道了 / 我明白了 / 我懂了 (=Yes, I know.) 是英美人士经常用的口头语。

2. 中文"尺寸是390mm×230mm×45mm"翻译成："45mm×230mm×390mm" 读作：forty-five millimeters by two hundred and thirty millimeters by three hundred and ninety millimeters。在我国，我们经常用"长、宽、高"的顺序来描述物体大小；而在英语中描述的顺序是"高、宽、长"，所以在给西方客户介绍我们的保管箱时，需要把语序做相应的调整。

3. staff/employee *n.* 员工，职员，雇员。辨析：staff 侧重于表述"职员"的身份，常常指一个单位的全体员工，单数复数形式相同。而 employee 侧重于"雇员"的意思，指明雇员与雇主的关系，与其所在单位的关系。此处场景为我行员工与客户的对话，所以用 staff 更为准确。

Safe Deposit Box 银行保管箱业务

T: Terms about losing keys are contained in the contract. The renter should pay 400 Yuan for losing one key and 800 Yuan for losing two keys. Therefore, we suggest you keep the keys safe; otherwise, there is no way to open the box unless we drill it through and then make you new keys.

C: Well, I see. After finishing the procedure, how can I use the box?

T: It's easy. After registration, we'll give you an entry card. Whenever you come to use your box, you swipe the card outside the gate of our vault to get in, and then you log on our automatic identification system by entering a four-digit password on that machine. And if the password is correct, the system will direct you to the corresponding private room in which you can use the key to open your box.

C: Well, I see. Thank you, good-bye!

T: My pleasure, good-bye!

drill /drɪl/ vt. 钻孔

Banking English

补充单词

subsidiary	/səb'sɪdjəri/	n.	子公司,下属机构
the termination of an agreement			契约满期日
put away			放好,储存……备用
drill through			钻通,钻透
pull out			拔出,抽出,拿出

Exercise

I. Fill in the blank

1. You _____ _____ _____ today.
   您今天看起来非常高兴。

2. Would you please _____ _____ _____ this medal for me?
   您能帮我保管这块奖牌吗?

3. _____ can I get there then?
   请问我怎么才能到那里去呢?

4. I am sure you will _____ warm welcome and quality service in the taxi.
   我相信北京的出租车会为您提供周到热情的服务。

5. The Beijing Branch of your bank told me that the business of safe deposit box is _____ over here.
   你们北京分行的员工告诉我这里可以办理保管箱业务。

6. I want to _____ my medal here in the box while I am in Beijing.
   我想我在北京的时候你们能帮我保管这块奖牌。

7. _____ _____ your medal!
   祝贺您取得了奖牌!

8. Please _____ those terms carefully first, _____ _____ your personal information here and then _____ at the bottom.
   请您先仔细阅读一下条款,然后再填写一下个人信息,最后在下面签字。

9. Here is one copy of the lease agreement as well as the _____ of the _____ _____ and the guarantee deposit.
   这是合约和租金保证金收据。

10. If you lose both keys, you'll have to pay 800 RMB to _____ open the box and to change a new lock.
    如果您两把钥匙都丢失了,我们要收取800元用于凿箱及更换新的箱锁。

银行保管箱业务
Safe Deposit Box

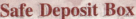

11. I'd like to _____ the save deposit box and _____ my medal _____.
    我想把保管箱退掉，把奖牌取出。

12. Do you take the _____, the _____ of _____ _____ and your _____ _____ with you?
    您的合约、保证金收据及证件都带了吗？

13. Do you provide _____ _____ _____ _____ here?
    您这里有保管箱业务吗？

14. RMB 1600 Yuan should be deposited _____ _____ _____.
    您需要交纳保证金 1600 元。

II. Translation

1. 请告诉我您的箱号。

2. 您贵姓？

3. 请您在这里扫描一下指纹。

4. 您想续租多长时间？

5. 我建议您将所有的文件都放在箱子里。

6. 您带护照了么？

7. 请您填写挂失申请书。

8. 我们将把您的保险箱冻结 7 天。

9. 下次当您回来办理解除挂失手续时，请务必带上您的证件和挂失申请书。

10. 请您出示一下您的护照。我为您核对一下您填写的申请表。

11. 没有问题，这是您的保证金 200 元。您的保证金收据我们就收回了。

III. Multiple Choice

1. I want to share my happiness with my _____.
   我想让我的家人分享我的快乐。
   A. relatives   B. family members   C. family   D. friends

215

Banking English

2. Please _____ your fingerprint here.

   您先来验证一下指纹。

   A. test   B. examine   C. show   D. cheque

3. The guarantee fee doesn't _____ interest.

   保证金不计息。

   A. generate   B. produce   C. account   D. plus

4. _____ about losing keys are contained in the _____.

   合同包含了丢失钥匙的约束条款。

   A. Words...paper   B. Terms...book

   C. Terms...contract   D. agreement...contract

第七部分 大堂经理咨询服务
Part VII Questions and Answers at the Inquiry Desk

银行英语
Banking English

大堂经理咨询服务—1

大堂经理致欢迎词

分行某接待室，外宾数名。大堂经理仪容端庄，态度和蔼，向各位来宾致欢迎词。

M: 大堂经理

大家早上好！欢迎光临中国银行！我为能够接待各位尊贵的来宾感到非常荣幸。

中国古代先圣孔子讲："有朋自远方来，不亦乐乎！"今天，朋友们从世界各地来到我们北京，欢度奥运圣会。这是世界各国人民的盛大节日。我们怎能不欢欣雀跃呢！

中国银行是2008年北京奥运会的官方银行合作伙伴。我们北京分行全体工作人员竭诚为参加2008年奥运会的奥组委工作人员、运动员、观众和所有来宾，提供优质完美的银行服务。

为2008年北京奥运会提供金融服务是我们中行人的共同目标，我们一定竭诚努力，出色地完成这项工作。同时，我们希望各位来宾也能对我们的工作提出批评意见，帮助我们提高服务质量。

如果各位有什么问题请随时提出，我愿我的回答能令各位满意。

我和我的同事们会努力使各位的来访愉快而有趣。

在此，我谨向各位来宾表示最诚挚的欢迎，并衷心希望各位的来访有所收获。谢谢大家！

NOTES

本小节中没有对话，主要是大堂经理在用较为正式的语言向外国宾客致以问候和欢迎。在柜台向国外的宾客提供具体金融服务的时候，我们可能并不一定会经常用到这些句子，但是，掌握一些正式的表达法，将中国银行积极向上的精神风貌传递给来往宾客却是十分必要的。上文中大堂经理说的每一段话，其实都可看作是彼此独立的话语，我们可以将这些句子熟记甚至背诵下来，在适当的场合使用。

Questions and Answers at the Inquiry Desk

Making a Welcoming Speech

Unit 1

At the reception room of the Beijing Branch, Bank of China, a duty manager is making a welcoming speech in an elegant and friendly manner to foreign guests.

M: Duty Manager

Good morning, ladies and gentlemen. Welcome to Bank of China. It's our pleasure to serve you today.

Confucius, a Chinese philosopher in ancient times, once remarked that "how happy we are, to meet friends from afar." Today, our friends have come to Beijing from all over the world to celebrate the great Olympic Games. This is a grand festival to all of us. We are very happy to have you all here.

Bank of China is the official banking partner of the Beijing 2008 Olympic Games. Our staff at the Beijing Branch will be able to provide quality services and financial conveniences to the Olympic committee, the athletes as well as all other guests and visitors.

It is our common goal to be the financial support for the Beijing 2008 Olympic Games. We will do our best to make it a big success. At the same time, your comments and suggestions are welcome for the improvement of our work.

If you have any questions, please do not hesitate to ask. I hope I can always give you a satisfactory answer.

My colleagues and I will help to make your visit pleasant and interesting.

Here, I would like to extend our sincere welcome to all of you and wish you all a worthwhile and meaningful visit here in Beijing. Thank you!

---

elegant /'elɪgənt/ *adj.* 文雅的,端庄的
Confucius /kən'fjuːʃɪəs/ *n.* 孔子
philosopher /fɪ'lɒsəfə/ *n.* 哲学家,哲人
ancient /'einʃənt/ *adj.* 古老的,旧的
celebrate /'selɪbreɪt/ *v.* 庆祝,祝贺
comment /'kɒment/ *n.* 评论,注释
improvement /ɪm'pruːvmənt/ *n.* 改进,进步
hesitate /'hezɪteɪt/ *v.* 犹豫,踌躇
satisfactory /ˌsætɪs'fæktəri/ *adj.* 令人满意的
extend /ɪk'stend/ *v.* 给予,发出,延伸

银行英语
Banking English

大堂经理咨询服务—2

介绍中国银行历史及标识

一位大堂经理正在向客户解释中国银行标识的意义。

M: 大堂经理　　**C**: 客户

M: 您好。请问您还需要什么帮助吗？

C: 我已经办理完业务了，我在欣赏中国银行的 LOGO。

M: 您对我们中行的 LOGO 那么感兴趣。谢谢！

C: 您能给我介绍一下好吗？

M: 你看，这个外形是中国古钱形状，代表银行；"中"字代表中国；外圆表明中国银行是面向全球的国际性大银行。这一设计，融汇历史，展望未来，体现了中国银行值得信赖、不断发展的品牌形象。中国银行这四个字遒劲有力，舒展大气，是我国人大副委员长郭沫若20世纪70年代末的题词。

C: 我知道他是中国的大文学家、书法家。

M: 您对中国的文化感兴趣。

C: 是的，我很喜欢中国的文化，尤其中国的书法。我到过世界很多地方，看到很多地方都有中国银行的 LOGO。确实很美。

M: 是的，目前，全球27个国家和地区都有中国银行的机构网络，其中境内机构共计11,000余个，境外机构共计600余个。

C: 是的，中国银行是国际性的大银行。

Questions and Answers at the Inquiry Desk

A Brief History of the Bank of China and Its Logo

A duty manager is explaining to a foreign customer about the logo of the Bank of China.

M: Duty Manager   C: Foreign Customer

M: Hello, anything else I can do for you?

C: My business is finished; I am just looking at the LOGO.

M: Thank you for your interest in the LOGO of our bank.

C: Could you explain the meaning of the logo to me?

M: You see, the logo's shape is a Chinese ancient coin, which is a symbol of the banking businesses. In the middle there is a Chinese character pronounced as "zhong", which represents China; The outside circle expresses that the Bank-of-China is a large international bank that provides worldwide service. This design, embodying the combination of history and future, symbolizes the brand image of Bank of China as being trustworthy and of continuous development. The four Chinese characters of Bank of China, which look vigorous and stylish, was written by Guo Moruo, who was the vice chairman of the National People's Congress in the late 1970s.

C: I know he is a famous writer and calligrapher.

M: Are you interested in Chinese culture?

C: Yes, I love Chinese culture, especially the calligraphy. I have been around the world and I've seen the LOGO in many places. It is beautiful indeed.

M: Yes, Bank of China has branch networks in 27 countries and regions all over the world, among them, 11000 are domestic branches and 600 are overseas branches.

C: Yes, that is true. Bank of China is a grand international bank.

银行英语
Banking English

M: 我们中国银行有悠久的历史,早在上个世纪初,1912年,就成立了。有近百年的历史了。1929年就在英国伦敦建立分行了。

C: 我们法国巴黎就有中国银行。我经常去那里办理业务。

M: 您是我们中国银行的老客户啦。巴黎是个优美的城市,法国是个有悠久历史的国家。

C: 谢谢您的赞誉。您对法国文化感兴趣?

M: 我很喜欢法国的文学。我知道法国顾拜旦开创了奥林匹克运动,人称他是:"奥林匹克之父"。

C: 全世界爱好和平的人们都知道他。衷心祝愿北京奥运会圆满成功。

M: 谢谢!

C: 再见!

NOTES

1. shape *n.* 形状、形态
2. symbol *n.* 符号、象征　symbol的动词形式是　symbolize 意思是象征、代表
3. character *n.* 字符、人物、个性

中国银行股份有限公司北京商务区支行
Bank of China Limited Beijing Central Business District Subbranch

Questions and Answers at the Inquiry Desk

M: Bank of China has a long history. It was founded at the beginning of last century, 1912. It has nearly a century-long history and the London branch was founded in England in 1929.

C: There is a branch of Bank of China in Paris. I often go there to do business.

M: You are a loyal customer of our bank. Paris is a beautiful city and France is a country with a long history.

C: Thank you for your compliment. Are you interested in French culture?

M: I like French literature very much. I know Baron Coubertin initiated the modern Olympic Games. He was recognized as "the father of Olympic Games."

C: Yeah, all the people who love peace know him. I sincerely wish the Beijing Olympics a great success.

M: Thank you very much!

C: Goodbye!

Banking English

大堂经理咨询服务—3

介绍营业时间和营业网点

一个外宾走向大堂经理咨询银行的营业时间和营业网点。

T: 柜员   C: 客户

T: 您好,请问您需要办理什么业务?
C: 您好,我想问一下贵行的营业时间,您可以告诉我吗?
T: 可以,很乐意相告。票据托收、本外币储蓄存款办理时间是9:00—17:00,天天营业。节假日停止办理外币兑换。在重大节日和活动时,根据需要还要进行调整,到时候我们要对社会进行公告。
C: 谢谢!我还有个问题想问一下。我在××饭店住。距离贵行较远,我住的地方附近有没有你们银行?
T: 您是在××饭店住。我看看(于是,大堂经理拿出一张银行业务介绍,在查找。并指给外宾看)在您下榻的大饭店,东边过一条街就是我们中国银行的一个网点某支行,离您住的地方很近,步行大约10多分钟。您看看这个标识(指业务介绍上的中行标识),一过马路,您就会看到这个标识了。
C: 那太好了。
T: 对啦。如果您只办理外币兑换业务,在您下榻的大饭店就有外币兑换点,很方便。给您这张业务介绍,这里有我们的营业网点地址和联系电话。它对您会有帮助的。
C: 谢谢!
T: 不客气。

Notes

- business hours 营业时间
- close ... service/ stop ... service 停止营业,停止……交易
- at noon 在中午
- on holidays 在节日里
- put up a notice 张贴通知
- far from ... 离……较远
- ten minutes' walk 走路十分钟
- ten minutes' drive 开车十分钟
- logo 标志
- exchange agent 外币兑换点
- cross the street 穿过马路

Telling Customers about Business Hours and Offices

A foreign guest walks towards a service manager and asks him about business hours and offices of our bank.

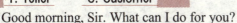
T: Teller   C: Customer

T: Good morning, Sir. What can I do for you?

C: Good morning! Could you tell me the business hours of your bank please?

T: Yes, my pleasure. Our business hours for collection of bills, Chinese and foreign currency deposits are from 9 am to 5 pm everyday. During important holidays and activities, the time will be adjusted accordingly. We will put up a notice at our bank then.

C: Thank you! And I have another question. I am staying in Garden hotel, which is far from your bank. Is there any bank close to my hotel?

T: You're staying at Garden hotel. Let me see. (the service manager takes out a list of banks and shows it to the foreign guest) There is a sub-branch close to your hotel. It is on the next street east of your hotel, about ten minutes' walk. Please look at this logo (pointing at the logo of Bank of China), you'll find this logo after crossing the street.

C: That'll be great.

T: Oh, yes. We have an exchange agent in your hotel, which is very convenient for you to exchange foreign currency notes. Here is an introduction to our bank business and you'll find the addresses and telephone numbers of our sub-branches on it. I'm sure it'll be helpful to you.

C: Thank you!

T: You're welcome.

银行英语
Banking English

大堂经理咨询服务—4

银行员工引导客户

中国银行北京分行的营业大厅里,办理业务的中外宾客熙熙攘攘。一外国宾客疾步走入分行营业大厅,迎面走来一位分行员工,他们彼此友好地示意问好。该员工英文口语较一般,对外宾提出的业务问题也不甚了解,于是他负责引导,请大堂经理解答有关问题。

B: 柜员　C: 客户　M: 大堂经理

B: 您好!
C: 您好!请问这里是中国银行吗?
B: 是的。请问您有什么需要帮助的吗?
C: 我是观看北京奥运会的希腊游客,第一次来到你们伟大的国家,我想多走几个地方。我让我的家人再给我汇些钱来。我想咨询一下有关汇款的业务?
B: 噢,很抱歉,我英语不好。我知道你需要帮助,但是对汇款业务,我也不太了解……
C: 对不起。我……
B: 没关系。我可以带您找大堂经理。他会使您满意的。
C: 好的。谢谢!
B: 不客气。请跟我来!
B: 李经理,您好。这位外国宾客有些业务要咨询。请您帮助解答好吗?
M: 可以。我会认真接待的。谢谢你带他过来。
B: 先生,这是我们的大堂经理,他的业务娴熟,外语也很出色,他会使您满意的。
C: 谢谢您的帮助。您能帮忙简直太好了。
B: 不客气。再见!

Questions and Answers at the Inquiry Desk

Ushering-in

A number of customers are doing banking businesses at the business hall of Bank of China Beijing Branch. A foreign customer walks in quickly and towards a bank clerk. They greet each other in a friendly manner. But the clerk does not speak English well, and he has little knowledge about the business the customer is asking for. So the clerk introduces the foreign guest to a duty manager for further assistance.

  B: Bank Clerk   C: Customer   M: Duty Manager

B: Good morning!

C: Good morning! Is this Bank of China?

B: Yes. How can I help you?

C: Well, I am from Greece. I am here for the Olympic Games. This is my first trip to China, and I really want to see more places here. You see my family is going to wire some money to me, and so, I am here to ask about the money transfer business of your bank.

B: Sorry, my English is not good. I know you need help, but I do not know much about it...

C: Oh sorry! I...

B: It is OK. Let's see our manager. He will help you.

C: That's all right. Thank you!

B: My pleasure. This way please!

B: Hello, Mr. Li. This customer has some questions. Would you help him?

M: Sure, I can help this gentleman. Thank you for bringing him here.

B: Sir, this is our manager. He knows a lot and his English is good. He will help you.

C: Thank you for your help. It's very kind of you.

B: You're welcome. See you.

银行英语

Banking English

C: 再见。

M: 您好！刚才，我的同事告诉我，您需要了解我们银行的相关业务。您能说得再具体些吗？让我试试能否帮助您……

> 大堂经理于是向这位客户解释了我行国际汇款业务的相关问题，并且帮助他开立了一个活期账户以便接收汇款。

C: 太好了！非常感谢。你们的工作人员真的很出色。顺便说一下，你的同事很友好，是位很好的年轻人。

M: 谢谢您的夸奖。我们只是尽力对来到我们银行的宾客做好服务。

C: 你们的奥运银行服务工作组织得真周密、细致。我们真有"宾至如归"的感觉。北京奥运会一定比我们雅典奥运会更出色，更好。

M: 谢谢。我们一定做好服务，把北京奥运会办好。

C: 我相信。这届奥运会一定会实现"同一个世界，同一个梦想"的。

M: 您真是太好了。谢谢您。

NOTES

在对外服务的时候，由于岗位和分工的不同，我们不一定人人都是英语专家，我们也不一定人人都是业务能手。然而优质高效的服务对于每一位银行员工而言却应该是人人追求的目标。本小节的重点在于，一位英语并不熟练，业务并不专精的普通员工(B)如何使用简单的英语，传递有效的信息，最终达到沟通的目的，使客户与大堂经理及时取得了联系。细看之下，我们会发现这位员工使用的英语词汇较为简单，句型也全部是简单句，没有漂亮的词汇，花哨的从句，却达到了有效沟通的结果，这种"化腐朽为神奇"的英语才是我们应该追求的。当然，文中的许多句子都是编者为了说明问题有意为之的结果，而且他与客户的谈话也并未涉及复杂的具体业务。同样的中文，我们当然可以用更加具体，更加贴切的英文来表达，在具体业务上，我们当然需要学习许多专业的英语词汇来构架我们的表述，但无论怎样，需要注意的是，好的英文不在于用了什么词，而在于怎样用词。

Questions and Answers at the Inquiry Desk

C: See you.

M: Hello, Sir. My colleague just told me that you've got some questions about our business. Would you please be more specific? Let me see if I can help you with that...

> The duty manager then introduces the customer to the international remittance function of our bank and helps him open a current account to receive the money.

C: That is great. Thank you very much. You are all excellent. And by the way, your colleague is very friendly, a really nice guy.

M: Thanks for your compliment. We are just doing our best to serve all the customers of our bank.

C: Your service for the Olympic Games is perfect and well organized. We feel at home here. I am sure that the Beijing Olympic Games are going to be more successful than the Athens Olympic Games.

M: Thank you. We will work hard to make the Olympic Games a success.

C: I do believe it! This Olympic games will surely have this "One World, One Dream" come true.

M: That's very kind of you, thank you!

---

excellent /'eksələnt/ adj. 极好的,漂亮的
colleague /'kɒliːɡ/ n. 同事
Athens /'æθinz/ n. 雅典

银行英语
Banking English

大堂经理咨询服务—5

叫号机的使用与银行突发事件的解释和处理

一个外国宾客走进银行，他第一次来中国银行办理业务，看到许多人坐在大厅里等候办理业务，不知如何排队等候。他走向咨询台问大堂经理……

M：大堂经理　　C：客户　　T：柜员

M： 您好。请问您需要什么帮助吗？
C： 我要领取从英国来的汇款。
M： 请您先到排号机前拿一个号码。请您跟我来。(大堂经理边说边带领外宾。)
C： 请您点击这里。(排号机屏幕上"个人业务")
M： 请您拿排号条。
C： 17号。
M： 请您在座位上休息一会，很快就会轮到您。到时，我会告诉您的。
C： 谢谢。
M： 不客气。

片刻，排号机叫："17号请到3号窗口"，大堂经理走上前请外宾办理业务。在办理业务中，突然网络中断了，银行工作人员和大堂经理婉转解释并及时处理这一突发事件。

Questions and Answers at the Inquiry Desk

Using Ticket Station and Handling Emergencies

Unit 5

A foreign customer steps into a branch of Bank of China for the first time. He sees a lot of customers sitting in the hall, waiting to be served. Being not aware of the queuing rule, the foreign customer goes to the Duty Manager at the consulting desk for help.

 M: Duty Manager   C: Foreign Customer   T: Teller

M: Good morning, Sir. What can I do for you?
C: Yes. I'd like to withdraw the money wired from the United Kingdom.
M: Please take a number at the ticket station first. This way please.
(The duty manager leads the foreign customer to the ticket station as he talks to him.)
C: Please click here.
(The Duty Manager clicks a button that reads "Personal Banking Business" on the screen of the ticket station.)
M: Please take the number slip.
C: No.17.
M: Please take a seat and have a rest. It will be your turn soon. And I'll remind you then.
C: Thank you.
M: You are welcome.

Moments later, the loudspeaker calls: "Customer number seventeen please go to counter number three." The Duty Manager goes to the foreign customer and reminds him that it is his turn.

The computer processing system of the bank gets disconnected suddenly when the foreign customer is doing his transaction. The tellers and the Duty Manager explain to the customer and handle the situation properly.

银行英语
Banking English

C: 怎么了,发生什么事情了?

T: 对不起。有点故障,请您别着急。我们尽快了解情况。您稍等。

片刻。大堂经理走上前向外宾进行解释。

M: 对不起,耽误您时间了。请您到这里坐。(边说边请外宾到 VIP 室休息)

C: 谢谢!

M: 刚才,我们了解了情况,是网络出了故障,工程技术人员正在紧急抢修,很快就会修好。

C: 相信他们会修好的。

此时,银行服务人员为顾客送上茶水、咖啡等饮料。

M: 请您用饮料,您是喜欢咖啡还是茶水?

C: 谢谢!我爱喝咖啡,来到中国,我更喜欢中国茶。

M: 您请,谢谢您。

片刻,网络故障排除了。银行又开始正常营业了。

M: 先生,现在故障已经解决了。请您继续办理业务。

C: 没关系,不要太自责。信息技术时代,人们越来越依靠各种先进技术和机器,因此,难免发生故障。我去过许多国家都遇到过这种情况,你们处理这类情况很好,反应很快,很有效率。

M: 谢谢您的夸奖,感谢您对我们工作的配合支持。欢迎您经常来我们这里办理业务。

C: 谢谢!

Notes

1. reliant *adj.* 依靠,依赖
2. transaction *n.* 交易
3. queue *n.* 行列,长队 *vi.* 排(成长)队,排队等候(up)
4. disconnected *adj.* 分离的,断开的,不连接的
5. 排号条 number ticket / number slip

    银行叫号机 Ticket Station

    理财室 VIP Room

232

Questions and Answers at the Inquiry Desk

C: Oh, what's wrong?

T: Sorry, Sir. I'm afraid there is something wrong with our processing system. Please don't worry. We will find out the problem as soon as possible. Please wait for a while.

Few minutes later, the Duty Manager goes to the foreign customer and explains the situation to him.

M: Sorry to have kept you waiting. Please come with me.
(The duty manager leads the foreign customer to a VIP Room)

C: Thank you.

M: We have learned from relevant department that there was a network system breakdown just now, and that the computer engineers are trying to find out the trouble. It will be fixed up soon.

C: I believe so.

Meanwhile, bank clerks serve the customers with tea and coffee.

M: What would you like to have, Sir, tea or coffee?

C: Thank you. I like coffee. But since I am in China now, I would prefer a cup of tea.

M: Very well, sir. Here you are.

After a while, network problem is resolved and the banking business resumes.

M: Sir, the problem has already been fixed. You can go to the counter to finish your transaction now. I am really sorry for the inconvenience and the waiting.

C: It's OK. Don't blame yourself too much. You know, in the age of information, people have become more and more reliant on advanced technologies and machines, and problems with them are hard to avoid. I traveled a lot around the world and it just happens, everywhere. But, you are good, quick and efficient.

M: I'll take your words as a compliment. Thank you for your understanding and cooperation. Hope to see you again. Good-bye!

C: Thanks. Bye-bye.

银行英语
Banking English

大堂经理咨询服务—6

接待友好客户并回答相关奥运问题

彼特·罗伯兹先生是个老客户,这天,他带刚刚从美国来的女友到中行办理业务。当他们得知中行出售奥运会比赛门票时,非常高兴。于是,大堂经理向他们介绍起了奥运会比赛和比赛场馆……

M: 大堂经理   R: 彼特·罗伯特   C: 玛丽

M: 又见到您真高兴,彼特·罗伯特先生。
R: 我也是。李小姐,这是我的女朋友玛丽小姐。
M: 您好!
R: 玛丽是特意来观看奥运会的。她的父亲从美国给她汇来一笔钱,我们是来取钱的。
M: 欢迎您来到北京,玛丽小姐。我们会帮助您办理这笔业务的。您们还需要其他帮助吗?
C: 谢谢!我们想问问哪里可以买到奥运会门票?
M: 除了运动场馆销售奥运会的门票外,我们中国银行北京分行所有的网点也代售。我们可以帮您预订奥运会的门票的。
C: 太好了!
R: 我想看8月20日在"鸟巢"运动场的足球赛。
M: 您喜欢足球!
R: 是的。因为这场球赛有中国队,我非常想看"中国队"的比赛,希望他们能有出色的表现。
M: 谢谢您对中国足球的美好祝愿,也很高兴您喜欢中国足球队。

Questions and Answers at the Inquiry Desk

Receiving Friendly Customers and Answering Questions about Olympic Games

Unit 6

One day, Peter Robert, a regular customer, brings his girlfriend from the United States to Bank of China for some business. They are happy to hear that the tickets of 2008 Beijing Olympic Games are sold at Bank of China. A duty manager then introduces Olympic events and stadiums to them...

 M: Duty Manager   R: Peter Roberts   C: Mary

M: Good morning, Mr. Peter Roberts. Nice to see you again.

R: Nice to see you too, Miss Li. Let me introduce my girlfriend, Mary.

M: Nice to meet you!

R: Mary came for the 2008 Olympic Games. Her father has just wired some money to her and we are here to collect it.

M: Welcome to Beijing, Mary. I'll help you with the money wired. Anything else that I can do for you?

C: Thank you. Yes, could you tell me where I can buy tickets to all these matches?

M: In addition to the stadiums, you can also buy tickets at the branches of Bank of China and all the sub-branches, too. We can help you book the tickets you want.

C: That's great!

R: I want to watch the soccer match at the *Bird's Nest* Sports Field on August, 20th.

M: You are a soccer fan, aren't you?

R: Yes. You know, Chinese national soccer team is playing in this game and I'd like to watch them play very much.
I hope they will have a good performance.

Bird's Nest 鸟巢

M: Thank you for your good wishes. Glad that

235

银行英语
Banking English

R: 我还喜欢"鸟巢"的建筑，因为她是自然美和独具匠心的建筑设计的完美结合。

M: 谢谢。"鸟巢"的建筑确实是独具匠心的。它充分体现了这届北京奥运会"绿色奥运、科技奥运、人文奥运"的理念。

R: 我还想陪玛丽看花样游泳比赛。你知道在哪里比赛吗？

M: 花样游泳比赛是在"水立方"比赛场馆。

R: 太好了。我这些天一直想看看"水立方"场馆。这个建筑肯定也很有浪漫情调。在这里比赛花样游泳一定很诱人。

M: 是的。这个比赛场馆和体育比赛项目和谐统一，融为一体，肯定很有吸引力。您绝对不能错过。

C: 我们会很高兴地观看奥运会的比赛，愉快地度过每一天的。

M: 祝愿您们快乐。5号窗口出售比赛门票。楼上VIP理财客户经理还准备了奥运会比赛"套餐"，您们不妨看看，然后作出更好的选择。

C: 谢谢！

M: 不客气。

NOTES

1. look forward to 期望，等待。介词"to"后面应接名词或是动词的 -ing 形式

   e.g. I am really looking forward to the party.

   我一直就对那个聚会很期待。

   e.g. I am looking forward to watching this game.

   我期待着观看这场比赛。

2. 当别人对我们表示赞扬的时候，我们习惯的反应是谦虚严谨地表达，例如当别人赞扬我们英语讲得好时，我们或许会谦虚地说："哪里，哪里，我的口语其实不值一提。"这是我们东方人谦和善良的表现。但是在外国朋友对我们表示赞扬的时候，我们有时尽可以大方地说声谢谢，表示对对方意见的尊重及认同。例如，同样面对那句"Your English is really good. 你英语讲得很好。"我们就可以说："Thanks. I do practice a lot. 谢谢，这是我经常练习的结果。"当然，我们还可以在后面加上一句"but I am still learning. 但是我还需要继续学习。"这样，仍然不失我们谦和的东方风度。对话中，当外国客人对我们的奥运场馆、特色建筑以及运动员进行褒扬的时候，大堂经理就表现得落落大方。她直接回应了客户的赞扬，进一步解说加深了客户的印象，增添了他们对奥运的期待感，最终成功营销了奥运产品。试想，如果客户满是期待地说"I'd like to watch the Chinese national soccer team play very much. 我真的很想看中国足球队的比赛。"我们却回应说："Oh, really?! They suck! 啊？真的？他们简直糟透了！"结果会怎么样呢？再比如，当客人赞扬我们的奥运场馆匠心独具，构造迷人时，我们却"谦虚"地回应："No, no, that means nothing. 不，不，那可没什么了不起。"客户还会那么热情主动地购买奥运比赛入场券吗？总之，在面对外国客人友好的赞美时，我们大可不必拘谨，充满自信地说声"Thanks！"才是好的选择。

Questions and Answers at the Inquiry Desk

you like the Chinese soccer team.

R: The structure of the *Bird's Nest* is also my favorite. It is a perfect combination of natural beauty and architectural genius.

M: Thanks. The architecture of the *Bird's Nest* does have its unique style. It fully reflects the concept of the 2008 Beijing Olympic Games, like, you know, Green Olympics, High-Tech Olympics and People's Olympics.

R: Mary and I also want to watch the synchronized swimming. Do you know where it will be?

M: Synchronized swimming will be held at *The Water Cube* venue.

R: Sounds amazing. I've been looking forward to seeing *The Water Cube* for a long time. I guess the building must be romantic. Well, think about it, synchronized swimming girls in there, wow...

M: Yes, you are right. The sports venue is in perfect harmony with the swimming games. It has a great appeal. You just can't miss that.

C: We will enjoy the games and have fun while we are in Beijing.

M: I wish you a happy stay in Beijing. Oh, the tickets are sold at counter No.5. Besides, our VIP manger upstairs has a special booking package for match tickets. You may want to check it out and make a better selection of tickets there.

C: OK. Thank you.

M: You're welcome.

---

structure /ˈstrʌktʃə/ *n.* 结构，构造，建筑物
architecture /ˈɑːkɪtektʃə/ *n.* 建筑，建筑学
unique /juːˈniːk/ *adj.* 唯一的，独特的
synchronized swimming 花样游泳
The Water Cube 水立方
romantic /rəʊˈmæntɪk/ *adj.* 传奇式的，浪漫的
venue /ˈvenjuː/ *n.* 会议地点，比赛地点
harmony /ˈhɑːməni/ *n.* 协调，融洽
specialize /ˈspeʃəlaɪz/ *v.* 专门研究，专攻，擅长

银行英语
Banking English

大堂经理咨询服务—7

接待着急客户

大堂经理看见一位非常焦急的国外客户在柜台前徘徊。

M: 大堂经理　　W: 着急客户　　C: 客户

M: 您好,先生。请问您办理什么业务?您看上去挺着急的。
W: 是的。我要乘下午4点半的班机,去海南参加一个重要的会议,现在还有1个小时40分钟,时间很紧。必须在10分钟之内办好取款手续,否则我就赶不上飞机了。我以为你们这里人不多呢。可是,你瞧,我前面仍有三个人,我不知道如何才能快点办完。
M: 好吧。请别着急。让我帮您办好此事。

M: 很抱歉打扰您们,诸位先生。这位年轻人有急事,他要赶飞机。我们想提前给他办理业务,各位不会介意吧?
C: 没问题,请尽快办理就是。
M: 非常感谢大家的合作。
M: 您这边请。
W: 非常感谢。
M: 别客气。这是我们应该做的。

NOTES

1. by air / plane 坐飞机　类似的表达还有:
　 by train 坐火车　by bus 坐公车　by boat 坐船 等
2. within ten minutes 10分钟之内

Questions and Answers at the Inquiry Desk

Receiving a Worried Customer

A duty manager sees a worried foreigner walking back and forth in front of a counter.

M: Duty Manager   W: A Worried Customer   C: Customers

M: Hello, Sir. What can I do for you? You look so worried.
W: Yes. I'm going to Hai Nan by air at half past four this afternoon to attend an important meeting. Now there is one hour and forty minutes left, so I am in a rush. I have to withdraw my money within ten minutes, or I will miss my flight. I didn't expect so many people here, but you see, there are still three people ahead of me. I have no idea when I can get it all done.
M: OK, don't worry. Let me help you with it.

M: Excuse me, gentlemen. I'm sorry to bother you. This young man is in a hurry because he is going to catch a plane. Would you mind letting him do his business first?
C: No problem. Please go ahead.
M: Thank you very much for your cooperation.
M: This way please.
W: Thank you very much.
M: You are welcome.

Banking English

大堂经理咨询服务—8

为残疾运动员提供特殊服务

一个下肢有残疾的运动员，从车上下来，我行为奥运会服务的志愿者，推着轮椅，走上前来。他们为残疾运动员提供特殊服务。

V: 志愿者　　C: 残疾人运动员

V: 您好！我们是北京分行的员工，是奥运会志愿服务人员。我们可以为您做些什么吗？
C: 你们好！我是小田次郎，是参加残奥会篮球比赛的日本运动员，请多关照。我的英语不太熟练，请不要见笑。
V: 您的英语很好，我们能够听懂，我们之间可以用英语交流。请您坐在我们的轮椅上，我们给您送到银行柜台办理业务。
C: 谢谢！你们辛苦了！
V: 不客气，为运动员提供服务是我们应该做的。

志愿人员将日本运动员送到银行大厅，大堂经理迎上去，表示欢迎，并为其咨询服务。

M: 大堂经理　　C: 残疾人运动员　　V: 志愿者

V: 李主任，这位是日本运动员。
M: 欢迎您，日本朋友。

Questions and Answers at the Inquiry Desk

Providing Customized Services for Disabled Athletes

An athlete disabled in his leg gets out of a car. Some Olympic volunteers of our bank come up to the athlete and bring him a wheelchair. They are providing customized services for disabled athletes.

V: Volunteers   C: A Disabled Athlete

V: Good morning! We are employees of Bank of China and also volunteers for the Olympic Games. What can I do for you?

C: Good morning! You may call me Koda Jiro and I'm a basketball player on the Japanese team for the Paralympic Games. Sorry I don't speak English well.

V: Your English is pretty good and we understand you quite well, so, we can communicate in English. Please sit on the wheelchair and let me assist you to the counter.

C: Thank you for your help.

V: You're welcome. It's our pleasure to serve you.

> Paralympics (Paralymic Games) 残疾人奥运会
> communicate /kəˈmjuːnɪkeɪt/ v. 交流
> wheelchair /ˈwiːltʃeə/ n. 轮椅

Volunteers take the Japanese athlete to the bank hall. The duty manager comes up to him, shows his welcome and answers questions.

M: Duty Manager   C: A Disabled Athlete   V: Volunteers

V: Mr. Li, this is a Japanese athlete.

M: Welcome to our bank, my friend.

银行英语
Banking English

V： 这位是我们的大堂经理李主任，他可以帮助您。
C： 您好。我准备兑付旅行支票。
M： 可以。请您先到贵宾室等候。我们安排有关人员为您办理业务。

此时，一名奥运会志愿者端着一杯茶水，送到日本客人面前。办理业务后，奥运会志愿者送日本宾客出了银行，并为其叫了出租车。

 C: 残疾人运动员　　 V: 志愿者

V： 您好！请您用茶。
C： 谢谢！
V： 请您在旅行支票的这里复签……您的业务已经办好了。
C： 谢谢！
V： 请问您下榻在哪家宾馆，我们准备为您叫"的士"。
C： 我住在奥运村日本运动员的驻地。你们志愿者的服务真热情，为我们运动员想得真周到。非常感谢！
V： 不客气。为运动员服务是我们每个奥运会志愿者的光荣。希望您取得优异成绩。
C： 谢谢！

NOTES

1. customized service 特殊服务，量身订制的服务
2. call a taxi/cab 叫出租车
3. come up to sb. 走向某人

中国银行股份有限公司北京西城支行
Bank of China Limited Beijing Xicheng Subbranch

Questions and Answers at the Inquiry Desk

V: This is our duty manager, Mr. Li, and he will help you.

C: Hello, I want to cash my traveler's cheques.

M: OK. Please wait in our VIP room first and I'll arrange to have your transactions done immediately.

At this moment, a volunteer brings a cup of tea to the Japanese guest. After he finishes the transactions, volunteers accompany him out of the bank and call a taxi for him.

C: A Disabled Athlete　　V: Volunteers

V: Hello, Sir, Please have some tea.

C: Thank you!

V: Please countersign your traveler's cheques here... Your business is done.

C: Thank you!

V: Would you tell us which hotel you are staying at so that we can call a taxi for you?

C: I'm living in the residential area for Japanese athletes in Olympic Village. You are warm-hearted volunteers and I really appreciate your consideration. Thank you very much.

V: You're welcome. It's an honor for us volunteers to provide services to the athletes. We hope you will win the games.

C: Thank you!

---

residential /ˌreziˈdenʃəl/ adj. 住宅的
warm-hearted /wɔːmˈhɑːtɪd/ adj. 热心的
appreciate /əˈpriːʃieɪt/ v. 感激,欣赏,赞赏
consideration /kənˌsɪdəˈreɪʃən/ n. 考虑,体谅

银行英语
Banking English

补充单词

duplicate	/'djuːplikeit/	adj.	复制的,副的,两重的
facility	/fə'siliti/	n.	设备,工具,设施
spectator	/spek'teitə/	n.	观众(指比赛或表演)
aspiration	/ˌæspə'reiʃən/	n.	期望,渴望
oral	/'ɔːrəl/	adj.	口语的,口头的
relevant	/'relivənt/	adj.	相关的,相应的
express	/ik'spres/	v.	表达,表示
mention	/'menʃən/	v.	提及,说起
professional	/prə'feʃənəl/	adj.	专业的,职业的
familiar	/fə'miljə/	adj.	熟悉的,了解的
responsible	/ri'spɒnsəbəl/	adj.	负责任的,可靠的
warmhearted	/wɔːm'hɑːtid/	adj.	热心肠的
thoughtful	/'θɔːtfəl/	adj.	体贴的,关切的
encouragement	/in'kʌridʒmənt/	n.	鼓励,奖励
embody	/im'bɒdi/	v.	具体表达,使具体化,包含
concept	/'kɔnsept/	n.	观念,概念
forgive	/fə'giv/	v.	原谅

Exercise

I. Fill in the blank

1. We _____ welcome you to Bank of China.
   热烈欢迎大家来到中国银行。

2. I want to _____ my warmest welcome to all of you.
   我向各位来宾表示最诚挚的欢迎。

3. I want to visit _____ places.
   我打算去更多的地方。

4. The clerk is not specialized in international settlement business, and his oral English is not good _____.
   那个银行职员不仅不太了解国际结算业务,而且他的英语也不好。

5. _____ _____ denominations do you have?
   请问都有多少种面额?

Questions and Answers at the Inquiry Desk

6. _____ _____ twelve denominations.
   一共有 12 种面额。

7. Would you mind _____ his business first.
   你们介意先为他办理业务吗？

8. I have to withdraw my money _____ ten minutes.
   我要在十分钟之内取好钱。

9. Time is _____ for me.
   时间对我来说很有限。

10. We are _____ of Bank of China.
    我们是中国银行的员工。

11. Please _____ me my poor English.
    我的英语不好，请不要介意。

12. We are _____ to _____ in English.
    我们可以用英语交流。

II. Multiple choice

1. I'd like to have my family _____ some money to me.
   我让我的家人给我汇些钱来。
   A. to remit   B. remits   C. remit   D. remitting

2. I am a beginner _____ English.
   我初学英语。
   A. in   B. on   C. for   D. at

3. What is the local currency here in China?
   中国的本国货币是什么？
   A. Renminbi   B. US dollars
   C. Pound Sterling   D. Japanese Yen

4. What is the unit of the RMB?
   人民币的单位是什么？
   A. Yuan   B. Dollars   C. Pounds   D. Cent

5. Let me _____ my girlfriend Mary to you.
   让我为您介绍我的女朋友玛丽小姐。
   A. to introduce   B. introduce   C. introducing   D. introduced

6. I _____ your compliment.
   谢谢您的夸奖。
   A. thank   B. appreciate   C. thank you   D. like

7. You could buy tickets at our branch and all sub-branches _____ sports stadiums.
   除了运动场馆销售奥运会的门票外，我们中行所有的网点也销售。
   A. besides   B. except   C. beside   D. except for

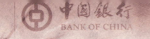

银行英语
Banking English

III. Translation

1. 中国银行是2008年北京奥运会银行合作伙伴。
   _____

2. 我们会尽我们的努力让您们的来访愉快而有趣。
   _____

3. 我不知道怎么表达我自己的意思。
   _____

4. 我们将尽我们的所能服务好银行里的每位客户。
   _____

5. 北京奥运会一定比我们雅典奥运会更出色,更好。
   _____

6. 我们想问问哪里可以买到奥运会门票?
   _____

7. 它充分体现了这届北京奥运会的理念。
   _____

补充阅读资料
Supplementary Reading

补充阅读资料—1

解释奥运会门票售票办法–1

2007年6月30日前的某日。一个在京居住工作的德国人，来到中国银行准备办理2008年北京奥运会门票预定手续。

C: 德国人士　**M:** 大堂经理

M: 您好。请问您需要办理什么业务？
C: 你们这里办理奥运会门票吗？我想订购2008年北京奥运会的门票。
M: 是的，您在我们中国银行任意一个网点都可以领取到门票预订单。
C: 还有其他单位办理奥运会门票预定手续的吗？
M: 一共有两种渠道可以预定奥运会门票。一个是登录北京奥组委官方票务网站。请您看，它的网站是 www.tickets.beijing2008.com。您按照网站提供的表格，根据它的说明去填写。用这种方式很方便，有什么事情，北京奥组委会及时通知您的。
C: 那第二种渠道呢？
M: 第二种渠道是填写预定单。您可以在中国银行网点领取。一式三份，送交两份，其中一份是原件。您可以将预定单直接邮寄给北京奥组委。它的地址是：北京100007号信箱，98分箱，邮编100007。
C: 我可以把申请表交到你们银行么？
M: 您可以将填好的预定单交我们中国银行银行北京市分行138家的售票网点。

Supplementary Reading

Explanations about the Olympic Ticketing Policies–1

Unit 1

It's before the ticket application deadline of June 30th, 2007. A German living and working in Beijing comes to one Bank of China ticket outlet and he wants to order some tickets.

C: The German Customer   M: Duty Manager

M: Good morning, Sir. What can I do for you?

C: Oh, sure. Can I order some Olympic tickets in your bank?

M: Yes, of course. You can get the tickets application form in any one of our outlets in Beijing.

C: Can I order the tickets in other places?

M: Altogether there are two ways. One, you can submit your ticket application online. You see, the official ticketing website is www.tickets.beijing2008.com. You just go on the internet and fill out the electronic application form according to the instructions. It's quite convenient and if there is any problem, you will get instant feedback from the Olympic ticketing center.

C: What about the second one?

M: The second one is that, you just fill out this paper application form, which, as I said earlier, you can get in any one of our outlets in Beijing. The form is in triplicate, and when you finish it, you can mail two copies, including the original one, directly back to the Olympic ticketing center. The mailing address is: Beijing 100007 mail box, 98 sub-box, and the post code is 100007.

C: Can I return the form to your bank?

M: Sure. We have 138 designated outlets in Beijing which accept the ticket forms. Would you tell me where you live so that I'll find the nearest one for you?

249

Banking English

您长住在哪里？可以就近找一家中国银行网点。

C： 我在朝阳三里屯住，那里也有你们中国银行。

M： 他们那里也办理收缴预定单业务。

C： 我是环保主义者，为了节约纸张，我还是选择网上预定吧。

M： 对啦。您的护照，还有必须是六个月以上的有效签证。

C： 我持有德国护照，我是德国人，在中国一家中国与德国合资的汽车公司工作。我有个中国太太，她非常漂亮贤惠。我正在准备办理加入中国籍的手续。

M： 祝福您。我们欢迎您。提醒您一下，您办理预定手续，一定在今年的 6 月 30 日前办理。

C： 谢谢您。再见。

M： 再见。欢迎您再来。

NOTES

1. joint-venture 合资企业
2. nationality 国籍
3. feedback 反馈

Supplementary Reading

C: I live at Sanlitun. I think there is one Bank of China near my place.

M: Yes. That one is OK. You can submit your form to that bank.

C: Oh, no, I am an environment protectionist. I don't want to waste any paper, so I'll go for the internet.

M: Good choice! And another thing, to order the tickets, you will need a passport and a Chinese visa valid for more than 6 months.

C: Sure, I am a German and I have my passport here and I am working for an auto company in Beijing, a joint-venture between Germany and China. I have a Chinese wife. She is a wonderful woman. And I have been thinking about having a Chinese nationality someday.

M: Wish you all the best. You are most welcome! And please remember, if you want to order the tickets, please do it before June 30th, because that is the deadline.

C: Thank you very much. Good bye!

M: Good Bye! Hope to see you next time!

银行英语
Banking English

补充阅读资料—2

解释奥运会门票售票办法-2

2008年5月,北京奥运会临近,一个外国游客向中国银行大堂经理咨询奥运会门票销售办法。

 C: 客户   M: 大堂经理

M: 您好。请问您需要办理什么业务?

C: 听说,中国银行卖奥运会门票。我是中国银行的老客户。我愿意在你们这里买票。

M: 是的。我们中国银行在全国有1000个网点代理销售奥运会门票,北京有138家。我们这里也售奥运会门票。

C: 还有哪里销售奥运会门票?

M: 除了我们中国银行,您也可以在相应的比赛场馆现场买票,所购门票是热敏门票。您还可以通过奥组委官方网站(WWW.tickets.beijing2008.com)或是票务呼叫中心(010-952008)进行订票。

C: 我们如何付款呢?

M: 在您采用呼叫中心、互联网订票之后,您需要在48小时有效时间内前往我们中国银行的指定票务受理网点缴纳票款。您可以选择使用现金付款,但我们建议您开立中国银行的活期存折或者使用Visa信用卡,这样,票款就可以直接从账户中扣划,比较方便。

C: 太好了。我有中国银行的VISA卡了,我再准备办一个活期帐户。我是中国银行的忠诚客户。

Supplementary Reading

Explanations about the Olympic Ticketing Policies–2

It's May, 2008. The Beijing Olympic Games are coming soon. A foreign customer comes to a duty manager of BOC to ask for information about ticket-selling.

C: Customer   M: Duty Manager

M: Hello, what can I do for you?

C: Well, they say you are selling Olympic tickets in your bank. I come here quite often and so, can I also get some tickets here?

M: Yes. Bank of China is a ticket agency for the 2008 Olympic Games. Altogether we have 1,000 designated ticket outlets throughout the country and 138, including our bank, in Beijing.

C: Where else can I buy the tickets?

M: Apart from BOC, you can also buy your tickets at the particular venue box offices and, in that way, your tickets will be printed out immediately. Besides, you can go on the official ticketing website of the Beijing organizing committee, that is "www.tickets.beijing2008.com", Or, you just dial "952008", that is the Olympic Ticketing Call Center, where you can place an order for the tickets you want.

C: How to pay for the tickets then?

M: Payment should be made within 48 hours after you order the tickets either by phone or on the internet, but whichever way you choose, you can only pay for your tickets through the designated outlets of our bank. You can pay by cash but I suggest that you open a savings account with our bank or use a Visa card so that the money can be automatically deducted. That is more convenient.

C: Great! I have already got a Visa card issued by your bank. Still, I'd like to open a savings account here. Gee... I am really a big fan of your bank; you should really give me credit for that.

银行英语
Banking English

M：我们一定为您做好服务，让您乘心如意。

C：现在全世界这么多人来到北京，奥运会门票能够满足我们的需要吗？

M：是的。这届奥运会是历届奥运会参加比赛运动员和游客最多的一届。奥运会门票总的原则是：现场售票，先到先得。您要是有意愿，最好是尽快来我们这里买票。

C：对。我回去和我的夫人、孩子商量看我们最喜欢的体育比赛。谢谢您的接待。

M：欢迎您来我们中国银行买奥运会门票。再见！

C：再见！

NOTES

- Outlets 销售点 网点
- BOCOG Beijing Organizing Committee for the XXIX Olympic Games
  北京奥组委
- Call center 呼叫中心

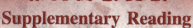

Supplementary Reading

M: Thanks. We won't let you down, sir. We'll do our best to give you the best.
C: Oh, you know there are so many people coming to Beijing from overseas for the Olympics. Do you think the tickets are enough?
M: Yes. I am sure that the number of athletes and tourists coming to Beijing will hit a record high in the Olympic history. So your tickets orders will be processed on a first-come-first-serve basis. If you've already made up your mind, just go ahead and buy the tickets here, the sooner, the better.
C: You are right. But I'll check with my wife and my kids first. We'll go for our favorite, you know. Thank you for your explanation though.
M: You are welcome and good luck for your tickets! Goodbye!
C: Goodbye!

补充阅读资料—3

奥运英语竞赛

中国银行北京市分行组织员工进行奥运英语竞赛。会场中央主席台男女主持人宣布"中国银行北京市分行迎奥运,奥运知识英语比赛,现在开始。比赛规则如下:必答题每队六题。每题 100 分。答对给 100 分,答错扣 100 分。抢答题三道,每题 200 分。答对给 200 分,答错扣 200 分。"

 主持人   两队队员

主持人甲:第一题。2008 年在中国北京举办的奥运会是第几届,将在几月几日几时举办。请红队解答。

红队 1: 是第 29 届奥运会。2008 年 8 月 8 日下午 8 时在北京举行开幕式。

主持人甲:完全正确。

主持人乙:第二题。2008 年北京残奥会是第几届,何时举办。请蓝队回答。

蓝队 1: 是第 13 届。在 2008 年北京奥运会之后约 10 天,按照规定举办残奥会。

主持人乙:完全正确。

主持人甲:第三题。2008 年北京举办的奥运会是在哪年哪月哪日哪个城市国际奥组会议通过的。请红队回答。

Olympic English Contest

Beijing Branch of Bank of China is holding an Olympic English Contest to its employees. The host and hostess standing in the center of the platform announced, "Now let's begin the *BANK OF CHINA CUP* Olympic Financial Knowledge English Contest. The rules are as following: there are six compulsory questions for each team to answer, 100 points for each question. You'll gain 100 points with a correct answer and lose 100 points with a wrong one. Besides, there are three timed questions with 200 points each. You'll gain 200 points with a right answer and lose 200 points with a wrong one."

主持人　　　两队队员

主持人甲: The first question. In which term and when will the 2008 Olympic Games be held in Beijing? Team red, please give your answer.

红队 1: It will be the 29th and the opening ceremony will be held at 8:00 p.m. on August 8th, 2008 in Beijing.

主持人甲: Absolutely right.

主持人乙: The second question. In which term and when will the Beijing 2008 Paralympics be held? Team blue, please.

蓝队 1: It will be the 13th. According to the regulations, the Paralympics will be held 10 days later after the 2008 Beijing Olympics.

主持人乙: Absolutely right.

主持人甲: The third question. When did Beijing succeed in bidding for the 2008 Beijing Olympics which was given by the International Olympic Committee? Team red, please.

Employee /ɪmˈplɔɪiː/ *n.* 职工, 雇员, 店员
Bid /bɪd/ *vt.* 出价, 投标

Banking English

红队2： 是2001年7月13日在莫斯科。
主持人甲：完全正确。
主持人乙：第四题。北京奥组委于哪年哪月哪日在哪地通过中国银行为2008年奥运银行合作伙伴。请蓝队回答。
蓝队2： 是2004年7月14日在北京通过中国银行为2008年奥运银行合作伙伴。
主持人乙：完全正确。
主持人甲：第五题。奥运会的理念是什么？请红队回答。
红队3： 更快,更高,更强。
主持人甲：回答正确。
主持人乙：第六题。2008年北京奥运会的口号是什么？请蓝队回答。
蓝队3： 同一个世界,同一个梦想。
主持人乙：回答正确。
主持人甲：第七题。北京奥组委提出把2008年北京奥运会办成什么样的奥运会。请红队回答。
红队1： 人文奥运;科技奥运;绿色奥运。
主持人甲：回答正确。
主持人乙：第八题。我行奥运工作的核心理念是什么？请蓝队回答。
蓝队1： 奥运创造价值。
主持人乙：回答正确。
主持人甲：第九题。北京2008年奥运会会徽是什么？请红队回答。
红队2： 是"中国印·舞动的北京"(显示图形)

Supplementary Reading

红队 2:	It was on July 13th, 2001 in Moscow.
主持人甲:	Absolutely right.
主持人乙:	The fourth question. When and where did the Beijing Organizing Committee for the XXIX Olympic Games (BOCOG) adopt the proposal for designating Bank of China as the Official Banking Partner of the Beijing 2008 Olympic Games? Team blue, please.
蓝队 2:	It was on July 14th, 2004 in Beijing.
主持人乙:	Absolutely right.
主持人甲:	The fifth question. What is the International Olympic motto? Team red, please.
红队 3:	Swifter, Higher and Stronger.
主持人甲:	Absolutely right.
主持人乙:	The sixth question. What is the slogan of the 2008 Beijing Olympics? Team blue, please.
蓝队 3:	One World, One Dream.
主持人乙:	Absolutely right.
主持人甲:	The seventh question. How will the 2008 Beijing Olympics be held by the BOCOG? Team red, please.
红队 1:	The Humanistic Olympics, the Scientific and Technological Olympics and the Green Olympics.
主持人甲:	Absolutely right.
主持人乙:	The eighth question. What is the key concept of our service for the Olympics? Team blue, please.
蓝队 1:	The Olympics create value.
主持人乙:	Absolutely right.
主持人甲:	The ninth question. What is the emblem of the 2008 Beijing Olympics? Team red, please.
红队 2:	It is a "Chinese seal, dancing Beijing".

> Slogan /'sləugən/ n. 口号，标语
> Humanistic /ˌhjuːməˈnɪstɪk/ adj. 人文主义的
> Scientific /saɪənˈtɪfɪk/ adj. 科学的
> Technological /ˌteknəˈlɔdʒɪkəl/ adj. 科技的
> Emblem /ˈembləm/ n. 象征

银 行 英 语
Banking English

主持人甲：回答正确。

主持人乙：第十题。第13届北京残奥会会徽是什么？请蓝队回答。

蓝队2：是一个充满动感的人形，它所表达的含义是残疾人在运动和生活中付出了巨大的努力。（显示图形）

主持人乙：完全正确。

主持人甲：第十一题。为迎接北京2008年奥运会，北京市民正在开展什么活动。请红队回答。

红队3：迎奥运，讲文明，树新风。我参与，我奉献，我快乐活动。

主持人甲：完全正确。

主持人乙：第十二题。中国银行奥运营销活动的主题是什么？请蓝队回答。

蓝队3：盛世奥运，百年中行，服务客户，创造价值。

主持人乙：完全正确。

主持人甲：现在红队和蓝队比分都是1300分。下面进行抢答比赛。

主持人乙：第十三题。中国银行奥运会合作伙伴形象大使是谁？

主持人甲：蓝队抢答在先。请蓝队回答。

蓝队1：奥运冠军杨扬。

主持人甲：回答正确。

主持人乙：第十五题。为什么我行聘请杨扬为中国银行奥运合作伙伴形象大使。红队抢答在先。请红队回答。

补充阅读资料
Supplementary Reading

主持人甲： Absolutely right.

主持人乙： The tenth question. What is the emblem of the 13th Beijing Paralympics? Team blue, please.

蓝队2： It is a stylized figure of an athlete in motion, implying the tremendous efforts a disabled person has to make in sports as well as in real life.

主持人乙： Absolutely right.

主持人甲： The eleventh question. In order to welcome the 2008 Beijing Olympics, which kind of activity is launched now by the Beijing citizens? Team red, please.

红队3： To welcome the Olympics and widely publicize the civilization, as well as bulid up new features and styles. I participate, I devote and I'm happy.

主持人甲： Absolutely right.

主持人乙： The twelfth question. What's the theme of the Olympic marketing strategy in Bank of China? Team blue, please.

蓝队3： Flourishing Olympics, centuries-old Bank of China. To serve the customers and create the value.

主持人乙： Absolutely right.

主持人甲： Now both team red and blue get the even score of 1300. Next, let's begin with the timed question.

主持人乙： The thirteenth question. Who is the representative of the BOC which is the Official Banking Partner of the Olympics?

主持人甲： Team blue hit the buzzer first. Please.

蓝队1： Olympic Champion Yangyang.

主持人甲： Absolutely right.

主持人乙： The fifteenth question. What's the reason that Yangyang was invited to be the representative of BOC which is the Official Banking Partner of the Olympics? Team red hit the buzzer first. Please.

tremendous /tri'mendəs/ *adj.* 极大的，巨大的
score /skɔː, skɔə/ *n.* 得分
buzzer /'bʌzə/ *n.* 蜂鸣器
champion /'tʃæmpjən/ *n.* 冠军

银行英语
Banking English

红队1： 杨扬曾在2002年美国盐城冬奥会获得女子短道500米和1000米两枚金牌。是第一个获得冬季奥运会的中国运动员。在她的运动生涯中共获得60多个世界冠军。并在国内外比赛中获得近100枚金牌。

主持人乙： 非常正确。

主持人甲： 请解释中国银行奥运合作伙伴工作理念"奥运创造价值"的主要含义。

主持人甲： 红蓝两队同时抢答成功！奇迹！（两队的灯同时亮起来）
请两队各拿答题板。用英文写答案。

红蓝两队各自答写。片刻。

主持人乙： 请红蓝两队各亮题板。

红蓝齐声朗读： 奥运创造价值主要包括：商业价值、客户价值、市场价值、品牌价值和员工价值。

主持人甲： 非常正确。

主持人乙： 红蓝两队各得1700分。

主持人甲乙： 我们祝贺红蓝队并列冠军！

NOTES

1. compulsory question 必答题
2. timed question 抢答题
3. Opening Ceremony 开幕式
4. The Paralympics 残奥会
5. The Beijing Organizing Committee for the XXIX Olympic Games (BOCOG) 北京奥组委
6. International Olympic Committee 国际奥组委
7. Official Banking Partner of the Beijing 2008 Olympic Games 2008年奥运银行合作伙伴
8. The Humanistic Olympics, the Scientific and Technological Olympics and the Green Olympics 人文奥运；科技奥运；绿色奥运
9. score 分数
   even score 平局   lopsided score 一边倒的得分
   level the score 把得分拉平

Supplementary Reading

红队1: Yangyang was the winner of two medals for the Woman's short-track 500 meters and 1000 meters in 2002 American Salt-Lake City Winter Olympic Games. She was the Chinese athlete who won the first gold medal in the Winter Olympics. She has won more than 60 World Championships during her athletic career and 100 gold medals more or less both at home and abroad.

主持人乙: Absolutely right.

主持人甲: Please explain the meaning "Olympics create value" brought up by the BOC which is the Official Banking Partner of the Olympics.

主持人甲: It's a miracle that both team red and blue successfully hit the buzzer at the same time.

Both you two please write the answers on the board in English.

主持人乙: Please show your answers.

红蓝齐声朗读: The values created by the Olympics include: commercial value, customer value, marketing value, brand value and employee value.

主持人甲: Absolutely right.

主持人乙: Both team red and blue get the score of 1700 respectively.

主持人甲乙: Congratulations! You are both champions.

Buzzer /ˈbʌzə/ n. 蜂鸣器
Congratulation /kənˌɡrætjuˈleiʃən/ n. 祝词, 贺辞

Banking English

补充单词

Platform	/ˈplætfɔːm/	n.	月台,讲台
Launch	/lɔːntʃ, lɑːntʃ/	vt.	开办,发动,发起
Civilization	/ˌsɪvɪlaɪˈzeɪʃən;-lɪˈz-/	n.	文明

Exercise

Answering Questions

1. When will the 2008 Olympic Games be held in Beijing?
   2008年北京奥运会何时举办？
2. When will the Beijing 2008 Paralympics be held?
   2008年北京残奥会何时举办？
3. When did Beijing succeed in bidding for the 2008 Beijing Olympics?
   北京是在何时申奥成功的？
4. What is the emblem of the 13th Beijing Paralympics?
   第13届北京残奥会会徽是什么？
5. What is the slogan of the 2008 Beijing Olympics?
   2008年北京奥运会的口号是什么？

附录一 (Appendix 1)

可兑换外币表 (Convertible Foreign Currencies)

代码	种类	符号	简写	面值	辅币及进制
01	人民币 (Renminbi Yuan)	¥	CNY	1,5,10,20,50,100	1CNY=10 jiao=100 fen (分)
12	英镑 (Pound Sterling)	£	GBP	5,10,20,50	1GBP=100 pence (便士)
13	港币 (Hong Kong Dollar)	HK$	HKD	10,20,50,100,500,1000	1HKD=10 xian (仙)=100 hao (毫)
14	美元 (US Dollar)	US$	USD	1,2,5,10,20,50,100	1USD=100 cents (分)
15	瑞士法郎 (Swiss Franc)	SF	CHF	10,20,50,100,200,1000	1CHF=100 centimes (生丁)
18	新加坡元 (Singapore Dollar)	S$	SGD	2,5,10,20,50,100,500,1000	1SGD=100 cents (欧尔)
21	瑞典克朗 (Swedish Krona)	SK	SEK	50,100,200,500,1000	1SEK=100 ore (欧尔)
22	丹麦克朗 (Danish Krona)	DK	DKK	50,100,200,500,1000	1DKK=100 ore (欧尔)
23	挪威克朗 (Norwegian Krona)	NK	NOK	50,100,200,500,1000	1NOK=100 ore (欧尔)
27	日元 (Japanese Yen)	J¥	JPY	1000,2000,5000,10000	1JPY=100 sen (钱)
28	加拿大元 (Canadian Dollar)	CAN$	CAD	5,10,20,50,100	1CAD=100 cents (分)
29	澳大利亚元 (Australian Dollar)	A$	AUD	5,10,20,50,100	1AUD=100 cents (分)
38	欧元 (Euro)	€	EUR	5,10,20,50,100,200,500	1EUR=100 cents (分)
81	澳门元 (Macao Pataca)	PAT	MOP	10,20,50,100,500,1000	1MOP=100 avos (分)
82	菲律宾比索 (Philippine Peso)	PHP	PHP	10,20,50,100,200,500,1000	1PHP=100 centavos (分)
84	泰国铢 (Thai Baht)	THB	THB	50,100,500,1000	1THP=100 satang (萨当)
88	韩元 (Korean Won)	WON	KRW	1000,5000,10000	

注：Krona 的复数形式为 Kronur

银行英语
Banking English

附录二 (Appendix 2)

国内外主要银行机构表 (The Primary Domestic and Foreign Banking Institutions)

	国内			国外	
国家开发银行	China Development Bank		世界银行	World Bank
中国农业发展银行	Agricultural Development Bank of China		国际清算银行	Bank of International Settlement
中国进出口银行	The Export-Import Bank of China/ China Exim Bank		亚洲开发银行	Asian Development Bank
中国银行	Bank of China		东亚银行(香港)	The Bank of East Asia
中国工商银行	Industrial and Commercial Bank of China		恒生银行(香港)	Hang Seng Bank Limited
中国建设银行	Construction Bank of China		淡马锡控股(新加坡)	Temasek Holdings
中国农业银行	Agricultural Bank of China		英格兰银行(英国)	Bank of England
交通银行	Bank of Communications		苏格兰皇家银行(英国)	Royal Bank of Scotland
中国民生银行	China Minsheng Banking Corp., Ltd		渣打银行(英国)	Standard Chartered Bank
招商银行	China Merchants Bank		汇丰控股(英国)	HSBC Holdings
中信银行	China Citic Bank		巴克莱银行(英国)	The Barclays Bank, PLC
华夏银行	Huaxia Bank		欧洲中央银行(欧盟)	European Central Bank
中国光大银行	China Everbright Bank		德意志银行(德国)	Deutsche Bank AG
兴业银行	Industrial Bank Co., Ltd		瑞士联合银行(瑞士)	The United Bank of Switzerland
广东发展银行	Guangdong Development Bank		美联储(美国)	The Federal Reserve
深圳发展银行	Shenzhen Development Bank		花旗银行(美国)	Citibank
上海浦东发展银行	Shanghai Pudong Development Bank		摩根大通银行(美国)	JP Morgan Chase Bank
厦门国际银行	Xiamen International Bank		美洲银行(美国)	Bank of America
浙商银行	China Zheshang Bank		美联银行(美国)	Wachovia Bank
徽商银行	Huishang Bank		三菱东京日联银行(日本)	Bank of Tokyo-Mitsubishi UFJ, Ltd
渤海银行	Bohai Bank		瑞穗银行(日本)	Mizuho Bank

Keys

第一部分　存取款业务

I. Fill in the blank

1. anything, open an account
2. Debit, cash deposit, withdrawal
3. update your transaction record, reflected
4. How long, foreign currency
5. The longer, the higher
6. fixed deposit
7. been remitted
8. sign

II. Translation

1. Please check up the amount in the deposit receipt.
2. May I get the money out before the maturity date?
3. I want to deposit the money in my current account with a time deposit certificate.
4. If you forget the password, you can only report a lost secret number.
5. The saving account is not allowed to be overdrawn.

第二部分　外币兑换

Fill in the blank

1. fill out / in
2. triplicate
3. exchange / convert / change
4. exchange rate
5. According to
6. leave, for
7. cash
8. counterfeit / forged note, confiscated
9. compare, counterfeit / forged note
10. concavo-convex, counterfeit / forged note
11. re-authenticate
12. show, passport
13. selling rate

Banking English

第三部分　旅行支票

I. Fill in the blank

1. international common practice, valid passport
2. countersigned, presence

II. Translation

1. The bank will cash you five-dollar check.
2. I have this 100 dollar check only.
3. Please show me your passport before changing your check.
4. You cannot entrust this task to anyone else.
5. Please fill out this application form first.
6. Do you get the authorization from your company?
7. We have to deduct a 1% of the face value discount.
8. The exchange rate for U.S. dollar is 7.8 to 1.
9. Can I change my money back then?
10. May I see your identification card? (ID=identification)
11. I need (some) change.
    =Could I have (some) change please ?
    = I'd like (some) change.
    = Please give me (some) change.
    =Let me have (some) change.
12. No small bills.
13. The ATM kept my card. (ATM: Automatic Teller Machine)
    =The ATM ate my card. (informal 非正式语)

III. Complete the dialogue

1. pleasure
2. traveler's cheques (checks)
3. cash / negotiate
4. countersign
5. passport
6. fill out / fill in
7. conversing / changing
8. exchange memo
9. How would you like your money?
10. souvenir
11. Wait a minute, please. / Wait for a second, please.
12. brand-new
13. My pleasure. / You are welcome. / That's all right. / Don't mention it.

第四部分　汇款业务

I. Fill in the blank

1. exchange memo
2. intermediary bank

Keys

3. value date
4. send the money, T/T
5. different ways, remittance
6. correspondent bank
7. According to / In accordance with / In correspondence with
8. inward / in-coming, outward / out-going
9. Identify, against
10. exchange rate
11. endorsement
12. account, branch
13. unconvertible
14. familiar
15. traveler's cheque
16. holder, deposit
17. issue

II. Multiple choice

1. A 2. B 3. A 4. B 5. A 6. B 7. D

III. Translation

1. I want to make some enquires about the requirements for outward remittance.
2. May I know which account you have in our bank, foreign exchange account or cash account?
3. I'd like to transfer money to my mother. But I don't know which methods I should choose.
4. T/T is the fastest way, but the service charge is also the most expensive.
5. Demand draft is the cheapest one among the three, but it will take long time to get the money.
6. You should mail the D/D to your mother by yourself.
7. I think my mother needs this money urgently, so I will transfer it by T/T.

第五部分　信用卡业务

I. Fill in the blank

1. withdraw
2. familiar with, introductions
3. compare, with
4. reject
5. deducted
6. According to
7. issuing bank
8. handle
9. contact
10. apply for, issued, Great Wall international credit card
11. regulations
12. initial pin number
13. Annual fee
14. monthly income
15. personal information
16. guarantor

Banking English

17. have / take a look
18. deducted automatically
19. authorization code
20. between

II. Translation

1. The principal plus the accrued interest will be automatically renewed on the maturity date.
2. Your credit limit is the maximum amount you can use every month.
3. We calculate overdraft interest according to the principal, interest rate and number of days.
4. Your marital status will affect your credit limit.

第六部分　银行保管箱业务

I. Fill in the blank

1. look very happy
2. take care of
3. How
4. receive
5. handled
6. store
7. Congratulations on
8. read, fill in, sign
9. receipt, rental fees
10. drill
11. return, take, out
12. contract, receipt, guarantee fee, identity certificate
13. save deposit box service
14. as guarantee fee

II. Translation

1. Please tell me the number of your box.
2. What's your surname, please?
3. Please scan your fingerprint here first.
4. How long would you like to extend your lease?
5. I suggest that you put all the documents in your box.
6. Do you have your passport?
7. Please fill in this application form for loss report.
8. We are gonna have your box sealed for 7 days.
9. Next time when you come to cancel the loss report, do remember to bring your passport together with this loss report application form.
10. Please present your passport, then I'll go through the filled application form
11. Well done. Here is your RMB 200 yuan for guarantee fee. Meanwhile, we should take back the receipt of it.

Keys

III. Multiple Choice

1. C 2. D 3. A 4. C

第七部分　大堂经理咨询服务

I. Fill in the blank

1. warmly
2. extend
3. more
4. either
5. How many
6. There are
7. doing
8. within
9. limited
10. employees
11. forgive
12. able, communicate

II. Multiple choice

1. C 2. A 3. A 4. A 5. B 6. B 7. A

III. Translation

1. Bank of China is the official banking partner of the Beijing 2008 Olympic Games.
2. We will make every effort to have your visit pleasant and interesting.
3. I don't know how to express myself.
4. We will do our best to serve all customers well in our bank.
5. I believe the Beijing Olympic Games will be more excellent and wonderful than the Athens Olympic Games.
6. Could you tell me where I can buy tickets of Olympic Games?
7. It fully embodies the concept of the 2008 Beijing Olympic Games.

补充阅读资料

1. It will be held on Aug, 8th, 2008.
2. It will be held on Aug, 18th, 2008.
3. It was on Jul, 13th, 2001.
4. It is stylized a figure of an athlete in motion.
5. One World, One Dream.